LORDS OF THE ARCTIC

LORDS OF THE ARCTIC

A Journey

Among the Polar Bears

by Richard C. Davids

Photographs by

Dan Guravich

MACMILLAN PUBLISHING CO., INC.   *New York*

COLLIER MACMILLAN PUBLISHERS   *London*

Macmillan Publishing Co., Inc.
866 Third Avenue, New York, N.Y. 10022
Collier Macmillan Canada, Inc.

Library of Congress Cataloging in Publication Data
Davids, Richard C.
Lords of the Arctic.
Bibliography: p.
Includes index.
1. Polar bear. I. Guravich, Dan. II. Title.

| QL737.C27D33 | 1982 | 599.74'446 | 82-10087 |

ISBN 0-02-529630-2

10 9 8 7 6 5 4 3 2 1

Designed by Jack Meserole

Printed in the United States of America

To Mae and Thomas and other seekers
after truth in nature

CONTENTS

FOREWORD

A Word from a World Authority

The polar bear to most people symbolizes the arctic, and, though they may never expect to see one in the wild, they want to know that polar bears are there and are being properly conserved. In the late 1960s, the worldwide harvest of polar bears was increasing at an alarming rate, and some thought the species itself was threatened. By 1967, public concern was strong enough to stimulate the five polar nations—Canada, Denmark, Norway, the United States, and the USSR—to start meeting bi-yearly to discuss international cooperation. From 1970 to the present, scientists from the five polar nations have met every two years to exchange data and discuss future research and management needs for polar bears. There was not always agreement on each topic of discussion, but there was unanimity in the desire to see the polar bear thrive throughout its circumpolar range.

In 1973, the International Agreement on the Conservation of Polar Bears was signed in Oslo, Norway. Each of the five countries agreed to conduct research on polar bears and, most significantly "to protect the ecosystem of which polar bears are a part." This polar bear agreement came into effect on 26 May 1976. To date, it is still the only agreement on any subject signed by all five arctic nations. It was to remain in force for five years. After that, if no country wished to terminate it, the agreement could continue indefinitely. In January 1981, delegates from the five polar nations met again in Oslo to evaluate the first five years the agreement had been in effect, agreeing unanimously that it had stimulated the kind of research and cooperation required, that the polar bear was not now a threatened species, and that the agreement should continue indefinitely in its present form.

It was out of the need identified in the late 1960s for more polar bear research that my own involvement began. I returned to Canada in 1970 from the southern hemisphere to study the population, ecology, and behavior of polar bears. I was less concerned about the protection of individual bears than I was about understanding the ecology of the species and protecting critical aspects of its habitat. Everywhere my colleagues and I went, we tagged polar bears to assess their population sizes and movements. I initiated new studies on the interrelationships between polar bears, the seal species they ate, and their sea ice home. In particular, I wanted to know such things as: How often does a bear catch a seal? Why do cubs stay with their mothers for two and a half years and what are the consequences of being orphaned at an early age? How do cubs learn to hunt? Can bears hunt better in some kinds of sea ice than in others? What sort of factors influenced changes in the distribution and abundance of polar bears in one area over the years? I felt we needed to understand some of these fundamental questions before we could realistically evaluate the effects of Eskimo hunting or man's industrial activities.[1]

In 1973, my graduate students and I began a long-term study of the behavior of undisturbed polar bears in the high arctic at Radstock Bay on southwestern Devon Island. We wanted to see what polar bears did when they weren't running away from Eskimo hunters and biologists—and we did! We had two small cabins about six miles apart and several hundred feet up on cliffs with commanding viewpoints. From there we could watch bears continuously through the twenty-four-hour day that prevails in the arctic during spring and summer.

We found that, on average, a polar bear catches a seal only once every four to five days. Most of the bear's hunting for seals was done by lying still beside a seal hole waiting for one to surface to breathe. Not once in all the years since 1973 has any of us ever seen a polar bear push a chunk of ice in front of his nose to conceal it, or use ice as a weapon by dropping it on a seal. We learned that polar bears sleep about seven to eight hours a day, just as humans do, and many other things that give us a much greater understanding of the relationship between this animal and its polar home.

Most of all, the seven years of watching undisturbed polar bears for days on end was a totally rewarding, even addictive, experience in itself. The sight of a large polar bear, glistening white in the sunshine, hunting seals by the edge of the icy blue water of a break in the arctic pack ice is one of the most spectacular sights in the world. An aggregation of five, ten, or more than thirty of these giant carnivores along the west coast of Hudson Bay in the fall is breathtaking. The suspense of watching a bear stalking a seal has more excitement than any movie. To watch an adult female traveling with her cubs, hunting for them, nursing them, and playing with them arouses the impressions of enormous strength, patience, and sensitivity.

Despite the many marvelous hours I have been privileged to spend watching polar bears, they are not easy animals to see, study, or photograph. In general, polar bears are widely distributed at low densities over one of the least accessible habitats in the world: the sea ice of the arctic. Although everyone knows what polar bears look like, relatively few people have ever seen one outside a zoo. In fact, many people who have lived in the arctic for years have never seen one. Probably far more people have seen wild grey whales or elephants. Consequently, to most people, even a glimpse of a polar bear from the window of a low-flying aircraft is exciting.

It is because so few people are able to see wild polar bears that this book is important. It came about through the dedication of Dan Guravich and Richard C. Davids, who have spent five years watching and learning about polar bears. It has been, they say, a labor of love. They have researched the literature well and taken every opportunity to observe and photograph polar bears undisturbed in the wild. More than that, they have interviewed Eskimo hunters throughout the Canadian and Alaskan arctic. A very special source of information was Ipeelie Inookie, an Eskimo who is as much a part of the arctic habitat as the bears themselves—but easier to talk to.

This book is, as its subtitle suggests, a personal journey into the world of the polar bear. It is a most enjoyable mixture of personal observations, well-researched background information, and new, imaginative photographs. From my own point of view, it makes a worthwhile contribution to our overall appreciation of polar bears in particular and to the arctic environment in the broad sense. I hope those of you who read the book enjoy it as much as I enjoyed reading the early drafts.

IAN STIRLING

Edmonton, Alberta

Bear-Watching

For two thousand years and more, the polar bear has walked the ice in a mist of myth and legend and superstition. Suddenly, out of nowhere, he looms beside you,[2] taking form from a flurry of snow, as illusory as fog and as haunting. Eskimos couldn't pause to study his habits or behavior; nor could early explorers. A bear at hand is a dangerous bear; in the arctic, there is nowhere to escape. So they shot him. Thus the polar bear continued as one of the least-known creatures in the animal kingdom.

It was this lure of the unknown that compelled my colleague, photographer Dan Guravich, and me on a personal odyssey for much of the last five years. By dogsled, snow machine, truck, ship, airplane, and on foot, we searched for polar bears, their maternity dens, and their temporary daybeds. The more we studied them, the more our admiration—yes, our affection—for them grew.

Dan first encountered polar bears in 1969, when he traveled as official photographer on the S.S. *Manhattan* as it smashed a way through the ice of the Northwest Passage for the first time in history. In eighty-three days, he saw twenty-eight bears, plus the tracks of a mother and cub who tried to climb aboard one night. Although I had spent some time among the Eskimos at Barrow in 1960, my first encounter with polar bears came in 1977; with Dan, I was on assignment from *Smithsonian* magazine to do a story on the bears of Churchill, Manitoba, where bears gather every fall to wait for freeze-up. Ice forms early offshore there, and ice to a polar bear means a chance to hunt seals; so bears gather there every fall to wait for freeze-up. During the annual influx of bears, the people of Churchill react with interest and affection rather than fuss or worry, and our respect for them has grown with every year that we have visited them.

What is it like to have bears at your doorstep, roaming the streets, sleeping in the schoolyard, and sometimes smashing through a window or wall? We have set down the inhabitants' stories. From time to time we helped conservation officers build trap sites out of railroad ties bolted into a **V** with a snare at the open end, baited with a cubic inch of blubber. After bears were captured, tranquilized, and tagged for identification, they were airlifted three hundred miles down the coast to be safely out of the way, but many returned within a few days.

That first year we came to know Ian Stirling of the Canadian Wildlife Service, Canada's top polar bear specialist as well as student of both arctic and antarctic ecology. More than anyone else, he has studied polar bears—their physiology, food habits, distribution, and behavior. From a cliff high above Radstock Bay on Devon Island, Canada, Stirling has studied polar bear hunting behavior, returning yearly to enlarge his observations. His colleague for several years has been Dennis Andriashek. Other young biologists are working with Stirling as graduate students: Paul Latour, with a master's degree in polar bear behavior; Malcolm Ramsay, studying for his doctorate on the reproductive processes of female bears; Mitchell Taylor, doing postdoctoral studies of bear populations in the Beaufort and Chukchi seas. We shared their hospitality and the comforting presence of their "thunder-flash" scaring devices, which explode safely over a bear's head. Never once while we were with them was it necessary for them to kill or even shoot at a bear.

On that first visit to the north in 1977, we also came to know Charles W. Jonkel, now at the University of Montana working on grizzlies, but at the time a leading researcher on polar bears. Together with his graduate students, he did much of the early work in refining the technique of tranquilizing.

During the falls of 1978 and 1979, we accompanied a Canadian biologist, Don Wooldridge, who is working to develop safety and warning devices as well as repellents.

In early 1979, Dan and I set out on a search for maternity dens. We traveled by dogsled through March blizzards that roared across the tundra, all but obscuring the dogs ahead. The temperatures were around 40° below zero. We built a snow-house the first night out; in the morning, the dogs were buried under drifting snow. Though we scoured the prime denning area south of Churchill for a week, we found nothing. We continued the hunt by plane and helicopter for a whole month, in vain. It seems that mothers and cubs had already left the area. Not until the following year did we finally find mothers and cubs beside their dens.

Also in 1979, we covered the high Canadian arctic from Baffin Island in the east to Barrow in the west, gathering data for several magazines on such topics as arctic botany and the effects of oil exploration. Naturally, we looked for bears, but though we searched for them by plane and helicopter over landfast and offshore ice in fjords, where Stirling had found them to be abundant, we saw no bears. We did, however, come to know a delightful young Eskimo, Ipeelie Inookie, philosopher and expert in the arts of the far north. You will meet him later in this book.

In Alaska that year our host was the distinguished Angus Gavin, educated in Scotland and now consulting ecologist to the North Slope oil explorations at Prudhoe Bay. We traveled with him from offshore islands inland to the Brooks Range, making a census of all kinds of bird, animal, and plant life.

At Juneau we spoke with Jack Lentfer, dean of Alaska's polar bear experts, and like Stirling a man who has given this manuscript a careful reading. Lentfer has tagged some eight hundred bears for his study of migrations and populations.

From Juneau we flew to Admiralty Island to study behavior of grizzly bears, cousins of the polar bear, under the tutelage of Stan Price, who for forty years has lived among grizzlies on his houseboat on Pack Creek.

In the spring of 1981, I visited all the Eskimo villages on the north and west borders of Hudson Bay, speaking with older people about the bygone days when men killed polar bears with no more than a spear or a knife. We talked at length about the spirit, or *innua*, of bears and other animals. No other trip of my life has been more rewarding. At Coral Harbour, where many Eskimos were out bear-hunting, Father Hubert Mascaret told of his life among Eskimos and his own hunting adventures. Catholic priests, as well as a few Anglican priests, have contributed immensely to our knowledge of the arctic. Father Frans Van de Velde, a Flemish priest who has spent his entire working life among the Eskimos of Pelly Bay, has written widely about polar bears.

Dan and I have spent long hours with these biologists, men of the cloth, and Eskimos. We have tried to disengage fact from fiction, reality from myth—which often isn't easy. Beyond that, we have made observations of our own. Though Dan and I don't feel like experts, we have observed the behavior of undisturbed bears as probably few other people have done. To our knowledge, nobody before us has photographed and described play-fighting, nor has anybody else seen a bear catch a healthy eider duck!

We did much of our bear-watching on a windswept cape on Hudson Bay from the safety of a "tundra buggy," a remarkable vehicle that can maneuver quietly almost anywhere over the tundra and coastal ice. Len Smith, an ingenious young man from Churchill, built it mostly with a welding torch. He took the differential from a front-end loader, the transfer case from a two-and-a-half-ton truck, and the transmission and engine and frame of an E600 Ford truck and welded them all together. Six feet above the ground he added a body nine by twenty feet and seven feet high. The tires are sixty-three inches high, and the whole thing empty weighs eight tons.

In the tundra buggy we could watch bears day after day without their being aware of our presence. For several weeks during both 1980 and 1981 we studied behavior. With us both years was Fred Treul, a Milwaukee industrialist, fine photographer, and splendid companion. On our 1981 excursion we had another companion, Fred Breummer, author and photographer of some of the best books ever produced about the arctic and Eskimo life, among them *Seasons of the Eskimo* and *Encounter with Arctic Animals*.

This book is a record of our five-year odyssey in the land of the polar bear.

OUR SPECIAL THANKS

A host of scientists and naturalists have contributed to this book, chief among them, Ian Stirling and Jack Lentfer. Dr. Stirling, Canada's top polar bear biologist, has studied the ecology of both the arctic and antarctic in broad-gauge research that includes interaction of the polar ocean and its ice and wildlife. His studies of polar bear populations throughout the Canadian arctic and Hudson Bay help determine harvesting quotas permitted Eskimo villages, and his environmental assessments guide Canada in its offshore drilling for gas and oil. He also participated in the polar research programs of both the United States and New Zealand and is a member of the Polar Bear Specialist Group of the International Union for Conservation of Nature and Natural Resources (IUCN). Jack Lentfer, a biologist in Alaska since 1957, has had both federal and state responsibilities in research and management of caribou and brown bears but particularly of polar bears. He was a delegate to the first international polar bear meeting in 1965 and to the Oslo convention in 1973, and has been a member of the IUCN Polar Bear Specialists Group from its founding.

We are indebted as well to Charles W. Jonkel of the University of Montana, one of the pioneers in polar bear research, and to Dennis Andriashek of the Canadian Wildlife Service. A hearty thanks to Angus Gavin, consulting ecologist of Alaska's North Slope, to Phil Howard, missionary and educator of Yellowknife, to Gary Laursen of the Naval Arctic Research Laboratory at Point Barrow, to Lawrence C. Bliss of the University of Washington, to John E. Sater, director of the Arctic Institute of North America, to John J. Burns of the Alaska Fish and Game Department, and to Ralph A. Nelson of the Carle Foundation of Urbana, Illinois.

We are grateful to the wonderful helicopter crew who watched over us on our search for bears at Brevoort Island, and especially to Bruce Eby of Esso Resources, and to our unforgettable young companion, Ipeelie Inookie of Allen Island. We appreciate the help of those fine Canadian biologists Don Wooldridge, Malcolm A. Ramsay, Mitchell Taylor, and Robert Nero; also of Father Frans Van de Velde of Hall Beach and elsewhere in the high arctic; of that master of the tundra buggy and mechanical genius, Len Smith, and of our other fine friends of Churchill, Brother

Jacques-Marie Volant and Lorraine E. Brandson of the Eskimo Museum, Joe and Lill Kowal of the Polar Inn, Keith and Penny Rawlings of the Arctic Inn, and that hardy Norwegian, Frits Oftedahl.

Our friends abroad, Thor Larsen of the Norsk Polarinstitutt, Erik S. Nyholm of the University of Turku, Finland, and Jørn Thomassen and Rasmus Hansson of Trondheim, Norway, gave invaluable assistance.

Smithsonian magazine, *Science Digest, Exxon USA, Alaskan,* and *Eskimo* gave us permission to use published material, Pocket Books permitted us to reprint short sections from the excellent book, *I, Nuligak,* and Philip Morris gave us permission to reprint photos. We acknowledge the logistical support of Pacific Western, Air Canada, Republic Airlines, and the Canadian Office of Tourism. For other fine help, we are indebted to Clive Roots and his associates at the Winnipeg Zoo, Terence Murphy of the Dublin Zoo, Christian Wemmer, curator-in-charge of the Smithsonian's Conservation and Research Center, and the splendid staff of Smithsonian's Natural History Library.

Our special thanks to Joyce Jack, who got this book going and saw it into print.

LORDS OF THE ARCTIC

O

Lords of the
Arctic

Striding across the top of the world like some ancient Roman god—both loved and feared—is *Ursus maritimus*, the polar bear, lord of the arctic, arbiter of five million square miles of snow and ice, a domain as great as Caesar or Genghis Khan or Napoleon commanded. From Siberia to Alaska and across Canada, Greenland, and the islands north of Norway, he is master of all living things, excluding only that sometime interloper, man. At ease with the brutal cold, the unending winter darkness, and the grinding, crushing ice pack, the polar bear rules in dignity, moving from one feast of seal to the next, a retinue of snow-white foxes following to feed on the remnants, with now and then a vagrant court jester, the raven, in attendance.

Ursus maritimus is big.

No predator on earth approaches him in size. Grizzly bears, especially those on Kodiak Island, average somewhat heavier, but grizzlies aren't primarily predators, since they live on grubs, rodents, and salmon, whereas polar bears survive almost solely by hunting seals. Polar bears are twice as big as lions or tigers. A typical adult male weighs half a ton and approaches five feet high at the shoulder. His paws are a foot wide. When he stands erect, he can look an elephant in the eye.

He is bold.

Even when we hover over him in the obscene racket of a helicopter, he often does no more than squat on his haunches and glare up, sometimes taking a swipe skywards. Most animals cringe and cower and run away from man. I have trailed tigers in Nepal, elephants and buffalo in south India, and black panthers in the jungles of the Therai below the Himalayas, and nearly always they move off. Not so the polar bear. It is a thrill beyond explanation to have an animal face up to you proudly but without hostility when you yell and flail your arms at it. When God told Noah that "the fear of you and the dread of you shall be upon every beast of the earth," it seems the polar bear wasn't listening.

More than that, he is beautiful.

His long, strong neck juts forward like an ancient gargoyle. His muscles, long and flowing, are ready for instant action. He glides across the ice with the same fluid grace as Joe Louis in the ring. His silky fur, generally yellowish white, may be

1

golden at sunrise and sunset, or snow-white in a blizzard. His muzzle is arched like that of a well-bred collie. He holds his head high like a haughty patrician.

But for all his dignity, he is fond of a good time. He dives into a meltwater pool headfirst and slides down a snowbank on his belly with obvious pleasure. He rolls on his back and kicks. A half dozen bears appeared to throw a party when they unearthed the cache of a scientist whose ship had been locked in by ice for two years. After feasting, they tossed supplies around like footballs, splintered a heavy iron-bound alcohol case, and ended up sliding down a long slope like children celebrating a winter vacation.

A cabin that polar bears have invaded is something to see. Bedsprings are ripped apart, bedding lies in tatters, the stove tipped over and pipes crushed, bottles broken, tinned goods torn or perforated with toothmarks, and any plastic materials shredded. There seems to be mischief in their makeup. In a final burst of fun, they smash through the wall to exit, even though the door hangs wide upon.

Polar bears love to swim. In summer, their intent may be to cool off. But late in October, a pair of three-year-olds who had been playing on shore walked and crawled across fifty yards of rough brash ice to glide into the water, where they swam among the chunks of ice with little more than their black eyes and noses showing. Then they came together to grapple and play. Often, one and sometimes both would be completely submerged. They disported like teenagers and, after coming ashore, slid on their faces and rolled on their backs, their black footpads waving as they dried themselves with the same gusto.

It is hard not to assign human attributes to the polar bear. He walks like a man, on the soles of his feet. He loves to travel, and sometimes takes off on prodigious journeys, just as the Eskimo does. He hunts like an Eskimo too. His home in winter is very much like an Eskimo igloo. And his temper sometimes seems human. A friend of mine once watched a bear on the tundra sneak up to a goose decoy and pounce on it. When he discovered it was only paper, he promptly stamped on and flattened all the others.

When two bears approach one another, they demand a proper introduction, as ritualized as an audience with royalty. One circles the other, ears laid back, in a kind of slow ballet movement. After a couple of circles, the two move nearer together until their noses touch, at which time they often sit, then open their mouths and gently clasp one another's jaws, heads atilt. If a bear is unsure about another bear, he will circle slowly downwind, where he may lie down and wait.

Bears, except during mating season, generally sidestep a fight. But after proper introductions they often start playing, which looks for all the world like real fighting. They pummel and push and bite, rearing to their hind legs. Adult females rarely play-fight, since they are accompanied by cubs and generally avoid other bears. Big bears are reluctant to play with smaller ones, but when they do, they are cautious about their pummeling. For all their size and strength, bears are gentle—incredibly gentle. Perhaps they need to be in order to preserve the species; certainly they have the capacity for quickly maiming or even killing one another. Sometimes a bear invites a reluctant bear to play. He wags his head quickly from side to side in a puckish, winsome set of gestures. The body language of bears is a pleasure to watch.

Even around food, there is little real fighting. When a small bear discovers a bit of leftover stew that we have thrown out, his growls generally chase off bigger bears. Prior right is important to polar bears. Again and again we have seen subadults chase away larger bears—until, that is, a truly huge bear moves in; then there is no further argument.

But bears are accomplished beggars, and often one ingratiates himself forward, worming his way on his belly, completely submissive, pushing himself with no more than his hind feet until he is close enough to reach out his tongue and lick the ice near the food. If he gets that close, though the master of the feast may growl and threaten, very often the interloper is permitted to feed.

Surprisingly, polar bears are generally dainty eaters. They carefully skin a seal and often take only the blubber, which they appear to love above all else. When we threw out a leftover salami sandwich a young male called Ossie carefully removed the top slice of bread and slowly ate the meat. Only much later did he return to eat the bread. When he and his sibling, Harriet, came upon a pile of year-old whale meat, they licked the oil and left the meat. Later, a ravenous young bear attacked the pile like a trencherman and gulped it down.

After eating, polar bears carefully lick clean their big paws, as a cat does, sometimes giving their face a few wipes with a paw. Much as they love blubber, they are reluctant to walk on it: They simply don't like having dirty feet. Their personal habits are fastidious. We have seen them back up to the edge of the ice to defecate in the water.

Rarely are polar bears hurried. They appear to pause and consider. If they are perplexed, they yawn. If they have nothing else to do, they take a snooze, often lying with the head resting on one incurved paw. Sleeping or awake, they assume any of several dozen other postures from comic to bizarre. When they want a better look, they rear up on their hind legs and peer ahead; one half expects to see them cup one paw above their eyes like a frontier scout. Standing at full height they are magnificent.

There is no end to the joy of bear-watching. Although each one is somehow different from the next, all of them, I began to notice, are bowlegged, as so many Eskimos are[3], and as they walk their front paws curve inward. Whalers used to call the polar bear "the farmer," from the way he plants his big feet firmly, deliberately, like a farmer going over ploughed ground. His legs are so covered with shaggy hair that he seems to be wearing a cowboy's chaps. As he claws up big chunks of ice as easily as if they were ice cubes, I watch to see if he is left-handed, as some authorities have stated. But the bears we observed used the right paw as often as the left, so that debate continues. On Banks Island, when Stirling and his crew extracted porcupine quills from a bear, they counted eighty-five on the nose, thirty-five in the right paw and none in the left.

Not long ago polar bears were thought to be loners, intolerant of others. But at Cape Churchill we have seen scores of them, big and little, in close proximity. Over the years we have repeatedly seen five big males lying together in the kelp, walking together, one time lying with all their noses pointed in and bodies radiating out, like a big white daisy, and another time concealed in adjacent dens in the snow, erupting as Dan's helicopter went over. (He took their picture just after they emerged.)

There are dozens of questions about polar bears to which we have searched for answers. Do they den up in a blizzard? Do they have their young out on the ice? Are they curious when they approach a human or do they regard him as food? That question has intrigued every traveler in the arctic. To help answer that question I sat in a wire cage at Cape Churchill while a succession of bears came past to look me over and try to get inside.

Just how dangerous are polar bears? That's a question we keep on asking. Within a few minutes after we made breakfast, half a dozen bears would move close in, lured by the smell of bacon. They would rise on their hind legs, their long black tongues lapping at the aroma, their eyes closing in a dreamy euphoria. And although the biggest ones could touch the bottom of the windows with their black noses, they seemed as safe—and as lovable—as a family dog.

But sometimes they didn't seem safe at all. On one occasion, at intervals all night, they pounced against the thin metal skin of the tundra buggy, trying to break through. Each time the buggy rocked, causing our gas lantern to swing wildly, we would unzip ourselves from our sleeping bags and jump to our feet, open a window, and shout. The bears simply reared up and looked at us. Dan was sleeping beside the gear shift lever, where a bundle of rags was stuffed around the lever's opening to keep out the cold air. During the night, a bear pulled out the rags from beneath and hissed in Dan's ear. As we lay trying to sleep, we wondered if and when the bears would learn to crawl up the sixty-three-inch tires, break the windows, and try to crawl in. Fortunately, they didn't.

We learned to recognize many individual bears. Some were tall and gaunt; some had big, sagging bellies; some seemed as square as beef cattle; some were creamy yellow, others were pure white. A small, four-year-old female, tagged two years earlier, had a scar above her eye like a penciled eyebrow. She, too, refused to be chased away and seemed everywhere present, necessitating a man on guard whenever we had to drop to the ground outside the buggy.

There was a young male that biologists had marked with a number on his side. He ambled from our campsite to Churchill, forty-five miles off, and three days later he was back again.

A giant old bear that we named Snaggle-Tooth frequently came close to the buggy. Like most older males, he was scarred about the face and easily identified. He was probably in his twenties and must easily have been five feet high at the shoulders, and, though he was so thin that his ribs and hip bones showed, the other bears still kept their distance from him. One long tooth jutted out from his lip; his jaw was broken during mating season and healed at an angle. Snaggle-Tooth seemed completely unaware of us as he climbed atop the trailer located several feet behind the tundra buggy and searched among the oil barrels for seal blubber that was once stored there. He tried jumping on Len's canvas-covered snow machine. Nothing that we tried frightened him away. He would leave when he was ready.

The veteran of Cape Churchill was a giant, incredibly thin old male that we called Split-Ear. One day he charged a helicopter at the observation tower, preventing Ian Stirling from landing. One ear was nearly torn away, one eye was blind. He seemed oblivious to us. How he managed to survive was a marvel, yet the previous year he was thinner still.

It is hard not to care about polar bears.

His Role in

History

For a wild animal living in so remote an area, it is surprising how often the polar bear has been front and center on the stage in history. Mankind, it seems, has had a fascination for—if not a love affair with—polar bears, going back to the days of the Pharaohs. The hieroglyphics from an ancient Egyptian tomb record an architect's plans for a burial vault for a polar bear. How these bears got to Egypt has never been discovered and barely guessed at.

The Romans, too, are thought to have had polar bears in captivity, which they turned loose with seals in flooded amphitheaters. Calpurnius in A.D. 57 wrote: "... *aequoreos ego cum certantibus ursis spectavi vitulos*" ("... sea calves also I beheld with bears pitted against them"). Since only a few fossil remains thought to be polar bears have been found below the arctic (at Kew Bridge, England; Hamburg, Germany; Hjørring, Denmark), it is likely that adventurous sailors braved the North Atlantic storms to bring the bears back from the arctic.

It was probably the polar bears' dignity and majesty, as much as their rarity, that made them coveted as mascots in the courts of kings. A Japanese emperor more than a thousand years ago was delighted with the two bears brought to him from northeast Asia as spoils of war; the event was carefully recorded in the emperor's annals for A.D. 858. Polar bears seem fit companions for kings, who "keep and esteem them as the greatest treasures of this world," according to an Icelandic bishop, St. Thorlak. Harold the Fairhaired of Norway was the first European king to have polar bears, caught for him by an enterprising hunter named Ingimund the Old around A.D. 880, when a mother and her two cubs had drifted ashore on the coast of Iceland. King Harold was overcome; he gave Ingimund an oceangoing ship filled with a cargo of wood. It wasn't long until every king in Europe wanted a polar bear. The king of Denmark outdid the king of Norway; for his bear, he gave a trading vessel, a sizable sum of money, and a gold ring. There were other less tangible rewards, too: in exchange for a bear, a canny priest named Isleif was made Bishop of Iceland, and Einar Sokasson, too, traded his bear for a bishopric in Greenland.

Emperor Henry III of Germany and his namesake, Henry III of England, each had bears as mascots at court. King Haakon of Norway presented one to Frederick

II of Germany, who in turn passed it along to the Sultan El Kamil of Damascus. Polar bears moved around Europe like chess pieces in a game of international diplomacy.

Throughout the Middle Ages, Greenland was famous for its polar bears and also for the greatly prized gyrfalcons, with which royalty entertained themselves in the hunt. Some of the earliest maps were drawn up to show not possible trade routes to the Far East (that would come later), but to indicate the sources of polar bears and white falcons! Thus both bird and bear contributed significantly to the medieval world's knowledge of geography.

Tartar tribes in northern Asia also traded in polar bears and their skins, according to Marco Polo, but the Vikings held a virtual monopoly. Swimming bears were fairly easy to capture, but in general hunters probably killed the mothers and took the cubs captive. They would spread the mother's skin out, and the cubs would come to lie on it, faithful to their mother even after her death. In Greenland, some hunters made rectangular traps out of big stones, with an overhead door that slid down once the animal was inside. Some of these traps still remain, the best of them on the Nugssuak Peninsula in west Greenland.

A bear at court lived a life of ease. It was Heaven, according to a sermon by the Icelandic bishop. "Almighty God," he said, "set two kinds of traps: one [for foxes taken for their skins] baited by the devil with passion and greed, whose trapdoor leads to death, the other [for bears] furnished with mercy and humility." So important were polar bears to the people of ancient Iceland that each animal coming ashore was carefully recorded. In 1274, for instance, there were twenty-two; in 1275, twenty-seven. A law book set forth ordinances governing captive bears: they must be treated as a dog and compensation paid for any damage they did; anyone harming a tame bear—unless it was guilty of wrongdoing—must pay compensation.

As well fed as these captive polar bears must have been, they were generally tractable, but they were also probably muzzled. An English king—obviously ignorant of the fact that polar bears do not fish—directed that "the sheriffs of London furnish six pence a day to support our White Bear in our Tower of London, and to provide a muzzle and iron chain to hold him when out of the water; and a long strong rope to hold him when he is fishing in the Thames."

Polar bear skins were prized for the altars and pulpits of cathedrals and churches, where priests used them to keep their feet warm. In Iceland, the king decreed that all pelts must be sold to royal officials, or elsewhere only by permission.

Hunters and traders slowly mapped out the intricate coast of Greenland and the eastern Canadian archipelago in their search for polar bears. But with the advent of Columbus a new age dawned, and the crowned heads found a new obsession— they must find an all-water trade route to the riches of Cathay.

But polar bears were not forgotten. One explorer after another couldn't help but record the big white animals in his log. John Cabot in 1497 says he found great numbers of them on Newfoundland eating fish; Jacques Cartier in 1534 saw one "as big as a cow and white as a swan" on Funk Island, feeding on birds that may have been the ill-fated great auks. On later voyages he regularly stopped there to lay in a store of birds and bear meat. John Davis, sailing for merchants of London in 1585, says he came upon "four white bears of a monstrous bigness." A handful of Dutch whalers spent a harrowing winter on Spitzbergen, with bears roving by their hut "in troops like cattle, making a terrible noise by their growling."

A Dutch captain, William Barents, wrote about his voyage in 1595 to Novaya Zemlya, islands north of Russia. One of his crew was collecting rocks that he thought to be diamonds when a big bear rushed up from behind and grabbed him. "Who seizes me so by the neck?" he cried. A comrade resting on the beach beside him lifted his head and looked, then jumped to his feet and ran, shouting, "Oh, mate, it is a bear!" The bear promptly bit off the man's head. Other men rushed up with guns and lances. The bear grasped one and killed him, while the others took to their heels.

Another sailor, whose ship was caught in the ice of Davis Strait, was hauled off by a bear but succeeded in making his escape by running off and throwing to the bear first, his only weapon, a lance, and then, one after another, all of his pieces of clothing.

The period from 1550 to 1850, when scores of wooden sailing ships floundered through the ice-choked bays and straits of the arctic, corresponded with a "little ice age" of worsening cold and weather. Henry Hudson in 1610 got caught in the treacherous ice of the bay that later would bear his name, and after a winter of near-starvation, the crew mutinied and set him adrift to die. Explorers in general lived on walrus and seal meat, but sometimes in the most violent blizzards, when it was impossible to hunt, they shot polar bears that came to their huts. "And right nice steaks and stews we contrived to make of them," wrote Walter Wellman, who led an expedition in 1889–99.

Eskimos largely died off during the little ice age, until only a few remained, living in a few bands completely cut off from the rest of the world. The so-called Polar Eskimos of northwest Greenland, in fact, believed they were the only people on earth. (Even the Tasadays of the Philippines knew that other tribes existed.) But in 1818 a British explorer searching for the Northwest Passage found them scattered over several hundred miles along the coast. Later, their knowledge of the arctic made them a mainstay to Admiral Peary in his search for the North Pole.

Whalers by now were killing bowhead whales and walrus by the thousands, flensing them of blubber and leaving the carcasses to be washed ashore, where bears would gather for the feast, as many as a hundred to a single carcass. Then walrus hunters began killing bears, especially as whale and walrus numbers declined. "In former times," wrote a Norwegian explorer, A. E. Nordenskiøld, in 1882, "the sight of a bear created dismay in polar travelers, but now the walrus hunters do not hesitate to attack, lance in hand, a large number of bears—as many as twelve within a short time." As the supply of hides jumped, so did the demand.

The white skins became the embodiment of luxury. No photography shop was properly equipped if it didn't have a polar bear hide as a background for some naked baby.

To explorers in remote areas, the bear continued to provide food. An Italian duke, Luigi Amadeo, journeying to Russia's Franz Josef Land in his ship, *Polar Star*, was forced to live periodically on bear meat. The best parts were the kidneys and tongue, he said, the rest being "not equally palatable." There was no shortage of bears; in one small bay, he and his crew killed thirty-four.

> Our dogs, which were so many, wandered about freely all day, pursuing every bear they saw. The larger she-bears were able to escape if they had only eight or ten dogs at their heels, but if they were attacked by a pack of thirty or forty, they were obliged to stop, and climb up on a hummock, or to range themselves against a block of ice by way of defense. We thus had time to come up and shoot them from a distance of a few feet. . . . We killed many she-bears, often accompanied by two cubs.

It was unnecessary to hunt bears: "A bear sees and smells a camp long before man is aware of his presence, and hunger compels him to approach."

There is good reason why such explorers were besieged with bears. Seal meat and blubber were food for men and dogs; seal oil was fuel for cooking and light. Every camp and man must have reeked of seal oil, which is extremely pervasive. It spreads like a fog over anything it touches, and persists for weeks. It is understandable that polar bears often mistook dogs and men for seals.

The Canadian explorer Vilhjalmur Stefansson, returning to his camp in the 1920s, sighted a bear that had begun to stalk his sled dogs, which were staked out near his tent at intervals of six feet along a tie line anchored at each end with chunks of ice. The dogs were too busy watching Stefansson to see the bear, which was only a hundred yards from them. As Stefansson ran towards the dogs he shouted, but this only distracted them more from the bear, which had moved behind an ice hummock for his stalk, hind legs bent so that he was almost sliding on his belly. Knowing that the bear was about to make his final charge, Stefansson could do nothing but shoot it.

Whether bears consider humans as potential food worthy of a stalk Stefansson wasn't sure. "It is possible that they would avoid men if they knew what we were, but they so frequently mistake us for seals that it makes little practical difference."

Stefansson spoke from experience. Once he had sighted a bear on the sea ice three miles off; he ran toward it, keeping watch of the topography behind him. At intervals, he climbed a high pressure ridge, but he could see no sign of the bear. He was just coming down the ridge when he heard a noise behind him like the spitting of a cat or the hiss of a goose. "I looked back and saw, about twenty feet away and almost above me, a polar bear. Had he come the remaining twenty feet as quietly and quickly as a bear can, the literary value of the incident would have been lost forever; for as the Greek fable points out, a lion does not write a book." The hiss, wrote Stefansson in *My Life with the Eskimos*, was his way of saying "Watch me do it," or it may have been a kind of chivalry, warning *"en garde!"* After a flawless stalk, however, the warning was a fatal mistake for the bear. Stefansson concluded, "No animal on earth can afford to give a warning to a man with a rifle. And why should he? Has a hunter ever played fair with one of them?"

Stefansson's defense of an animal that was out to kill him is a response typical of explorers. Polar bears were their companions-in-arms against the vicissitudes of the north; they felt respect and admiration for the polar bears, if not affection. There-fore, every encounter with a bear was worth noting. Admiral Peary's log book is crowded with such accounts. (Reading them, I think how richly aromatic with seal odor he and his crew must have been after months without baths or clean laundry.)

Sunday, October 7, 1894: The ship's carpenter spied a bear a few yards off. The man jumped onto a boulder, the bear after him, and fired a revolver from five feet away. The gun misfired, but dogs drew the bear's attention, permitting the carpen-ter to race for the ship. With the help of dogs, Peary approached within five yards and shot it.

Wednesday, October 31: Just after breakfast, someone rushed into Peary's cabin on board ship. The carpenter and others were on top of a log hut on shore, shouting. A young male polar bear had given chase.

Monday, November 12: Three more bears came to the log hut, one of them rubbing its nose on the window glass.

Tuesday, November 13: Peary was routed from his bunk at 4:30 A.M. In the bright moonlight, he could see a bear nearby surrounded by yapping dogs. He intercepted the animal as it tried to retreat to the bay ice. "He came at me at a good fast trot, and when at six paces off, I fired and he fell dead."

Wednesday, November 14: Another bear. "He showed a disposition to clear out, so I lay down on the ice and imitated the movements of a seal, quite taking him in, for he at once came running towards me, and when at ten paces off, I fired."

Friday, December 28: The ship's bell was ringing, which meant either a bear or a fire on board. Two bears had come to the ship. One man narrowly escaped being mauled. Both bears were killed. Nearly all the bears that Peary examined had no food in either stomach or intestines.

Thursday, February 7: On this day Peary's quest for the Pole nearly ended. Awakened by dogs at 5:00 A.M., he slipped on a coat and a pair of breeches over his pajamas. He fired one shot at a distance, then, to make sure of the shot since he had only one left, walked to within six or seven yards of the bear, which was surrounded by dogs.

> He rushed at me, at first with his head low down, but just as I fired he threw his head up, causing the bullet to go between his forelegs, and he came on at me with a menagerie roar, his mouth wide open, and in a second he was upon me. I could feel his warm breath upon my face, could see the gleam of his teeth and the shape of his long gray tongue, and the furious glare in his savage eyes. I had just time to remove the rifle from my shoulder, half dazed as I was by its flash in the darkness, and to thrust the barrel with all my force into his open jaws, and then drew it back for another thrust.

This was a trifle too much for him, apparently, as he whipped short round and took to the water, covered with thin ice as it was. My left hand which entered his mouth up to the wrist, as shown by the teeth-marks on it, bled a good deal, although the wounds were little more than deep scratches. . . . He was a good game bear, and I hope may have recovered from his wound. I have the greatest dislike for wasting life, and an even greater one to leaving a wounded animal to die.

The polar bear continues to interject himself in history. In 1978, the young Japanese, Naomi Uemura, traveled alone by dogsled to reach the North Pole. While his dog team slept, a bear ate all the dog food, then sniffed him over as he lay trembling in his tent. The young man seemed more awed by the bear than the fact that he had successfully reached the Pole.

World
Citizen

The polar bear is a world citizen, someone has said, neither communist nor capitalist, disdainful of national boundaries, crisscrossing the Iron Curtain with impunity. You might find him anywhere around the top of the world, wherever there are seals and ice and a little open water.

The ancestors of *Ursus maritimus* come from Europe, from the house of *Ursus etruscus*, the cave bear, the progenitor also of the grizzly, *Ursus horribilis*, also known, depending on taxonomists, as the barren ground, Kodiak, or big brown bear.[4] As late as ten years ago, the polar bear was given a separate genus, *Thalarctos*, but the fact that crosses of European and American brown bears produced fertile offspring returned polar bears to the genus *Ursus*.[5]

Perhaps some fifty thousand to a hundred thousand years ago—a mere yesterday in the flow of time—several brown bears may have been walled off by glaciers or perhaps some vicissitudes of weather shunted them away from the easier life to the south. Or did some bears simply prefer hunting to scrounging? At any rate, a race of white bears evolved, their color adapting as their hunting skills improved, and their teeth developing to better rip and tear their food. No fossil polar bears have been found that predate the last glaciation. Some scientists believe that polar bears are at the very beginning of evolving into a sea animal as comfortable in water as a walrus. Others say that his adaptation to water already represents a modern evolutionary breakthrough comparable to that of reptiles taking to flying.

The polar bear's body is more elongated than the brown bear's with a longer neck and a Roman nose rather than the dished profile of the brown bear. In keeping with its carnivorous diet, the polar bear's molars are relatively smaller and the canines longer. In size, the average brown bear runs one or two hundred pounds heavier. The color of brown bears varies considerably within the species, from deep brown, darker along the back, limbs, and ears to shades of yellow, gray, and almost black. Those in the barren grounds of the north are distinctly yellowish, even honey-colored. Polar bears vary in color from almost pure white to a pale lemon wash, but there seems to be no connection between color and location. The yellow color is not soil (as many zoo-goers are prone to think).

Size, not color, is what seems to differentiate polar bears in one area from

The travels of this world citizen may take him from one hemisphere to the next. Neither communist nor capitalist, he crosses the Iron Curtain with impunity.

Gentlest of the bears, he was
a companion of kings, and lived
as a mascot in palaces from the
days of the Pharaohs and on
through the Middle Ages.

Only in the last few years have
biologists begun to invade the
arctic to spy on this lovable,
fearsome giant of the frozen wilderness.

A creature of myth and mystery, he can look an elephant in the eye when he stands erect. To the Eskimos he was a shaman, in touch with the spirit world.

His land is a cruel one, but one with a haunting beauty all its own. An early explorer wrote: "A land that Milton or Dante might imagine—inorganic, desolate, mysterious."

Twice the size of a lion, he has courage to match. Though he may weigh nearly a ton, he can leap across great fissures, scale walls of ice that tower above him.

Gentle with one another, bears start each meeting with a formal introduction, opening the mouth and clasping muzzles in a stylized ritual.

Mother and cubs communicate with low growls and hisses. The cub at the left found a remnant of blubber and called in the others with a throaty rumble.

Ever on the alert, this mother is threatening an approaching male as one cub stands to get a better look.

Play among well-fed bears during autumn is an all-day affair as they wait beside Hudson Bay for freezeup. But first, there must be an introduction.

They grapple and push and lunge. We first mistook this play for actual battle, since no one before had described or photographed mock fighting.

Tempers flare for just a moment, but quickly cool. Real fighting looks surprisingly like this, but occurs mainly during spring mating time.

Big as they are, the bears move lightning-fast. We watched such shows for hours. They looked more real than human wrestling matches.

They stop only to cool off. Most bouts are between bears of about the same size. Adult females do not play, being occupied with maternal duties.

Bears signal their intentions with body language. A lowered head can mean aggression. This big one may be ready for a sudden charge.

another. The average adult male weighs about a thousand pounds, with females around half that size, and big males weighing up to fifteen hundred pounds. T. H. Manning, a Canadian scientist who has studied head sizes, notes that from east Greenland, where the skulls are smallest, the size increases westward to Alaska, where skull sizes are largest. Going east from Greenland to Norway's Svalbard archipelago, the skulls are bigger, presumably increasing all the way across to Alaska. The gradation in size, Manning believes, is genetic rather than ecologic, since he has found bears in the far north of Canada little different from those in the extreme south of Hudson Bay. Ian Stirling of the Canadian Wildlife Service, Canada's principal polar bear biologist and adviser to us for this book, believes that some size differences may be the result of variations in marine productivity but has not checked out his theory.[6]

The biggest bears have all come from south of the Bering Strait. According to the *Guinness Book of World Records*, the biggest bear of any species ever killed was a polar bear from this area, said to have weighed 2,210 pounds, and now on display at the Anchorage airport, where he stands eleven feet one and a half inches tall. Alaska's principal polar bear expert, Jack Lentfer of the Department of Fish and Game, and another adviser for this book, is skeptical of that weight. He has captured and measured more than 800 bears, and the largest he has ever weighed was 1,400 pounds. The hide of an Alaskan bear shot in 1961 measured eleven feet four inches from nose to tail; its owner maintains it is the biggest in the world.

Until recently, it was generally believed that polar bears were nomads, traveling without home ties everywhere about the arctic, global hitchhikers riding the moving polar pack like a merry-go-round, tasting the delights of one continent after another as they moved slowly past. It was a delightful idea but simply not true. Most polar bears keep to the same area in what biologists call populations. Alaska, for instance, has two such populations: one in the area from Point Lay between Wainwright and Cape Lisbourne west to Russia's Wrangel Island, and a northern group extending to the Canadian border. (There are no polar bears in the antarctic. The intervening ocean is too broad and turbulent. Stirling says that with all the seals and bird life there, they would certainly prosper; but introducing them would be an ecological disaster. At one time there were terrestrial animals on that continent.)

Mapping out the boundaries of each population is of more than pedantic interest. It is important to know in any one area whether bear populations are increasing or declining and thus evaluate the effects of hunting, mineral and oil exploration, and any change in food supply. There are even political interests. Do Russian bears overlap with Alaskan? Do Norwegian bears cross over to Greenland? Do bears born in Ontario get shot in Manitoba? Luckily, biologists now have many of the answers.

In the world, there are probably at least a dozen discrete populations, but within these there are smaller subpopulations of bears. Canada may have as many as ten or fifteen subpopulations, which occasionally intermingle. For instance, bears in northern Labrador, at the southern end of their range in eastern Canada, are part of a population shared with Quebec and elsewhere; some travel to Baffin Island and northern Hudson Bay. The subpopulation on southeast Baffin Island, however, shows a high fidelity to the area. Canada's gigantic islands and inland seas are certainly the world's greatest treasury of polar bears.

Norway's bears are on Svalbard, a cluster of islands to the far north, the largest of which is Spitzbergen. Svalbard is home to 1,300 Norwegians, 2,500 Russians and 3,000 polar bears, a figure estimated to reach 4,000 to 5,000 in winter when bears wander in from Russia's Franz Josef Land to the east and from Greenland to the west.

Denmark's bears are on Greenland, especially along the east coast from Scoresby Sound at the shoulder of the island and on north. They winter at the sound, where there is often open water, but migrate shoreward in mid-February when seals start giving birth.

Russia's principal bear country is Wrangel Island, which for a determined bear is about a week's walk away from Alaska. So these five countries make up the "polar bear nations": Canada, Norway, Denmark, the USSR, and the United States.

Most bears have strong attachments to an area. Those tagged off the north coast of Alaska, for instance, generally stay in the area, even though to do so means they must keep traveling against the westward direction of the prevailing ice drift. During spring, before breakup, they do move east searching for mates, feeding ground, and firmer ice, and those on the west coast move north, but they generally return to their home ground.

The fact that most bears have strong attachments to an area, especially to maternity denning sites, does not mean you will always find them there—much depends on the wind, for one thing. North of Alaska, when winds sweep south from the polar pack, bears riding the ice floes may be abundant. Likewise, when strong northeast winds drive great masses of ice onto the east coast of Southampton Island, bears may arrive in numbers; one Eskimo reported seeing 180 of them. Besides wind, the kind of ice determines where you will find bears. Seals have an easier time keeping their breathing holes open in ice recently cracked and refrozen than on thick plates.

Most polar bears are homebodies, yet—confounding all efforts at generalizing—some are wanderers. Sometimes they show up as far south as the Gulf of St. Lawrence and northern Norway, riding the ice floes on strong southerly currents. Not long ago a 1,400-pounder dropped in on the tiny fishing village of Indian Harbour in Labrador, as suddenly and unannounced as a traveler from outer space, and started breaking into buildings in search of food. Another traveled much further south and showed up one May day in 1973 just west of the beautiful city of St. John's, Newfoundland. Polar bears had probably been common there in the days of Erik the Red, but now, to the Newfoundlander, the appearance of the noble, unhurried creature was like a visitation of royalty.

Once in a while bears roam far inland. In the fall of 1978 one suddenly appeared outside Gillam, Manitoba, more than a hundred miles from James Bay. The same year, another showed up—like an apparition—at Norway House at the north end of Lake Winnipeg, no more than three hundred miles from the city of Winnipeg. Sadly, these wandering bears are shot by men who claim self-defense, or by conservation officers who proclaim that their first responsibility is to public safety.

It seems likely that such random journeys are part of a tendency for young animals of many kinds to ramble off, resulting in a dispersal of species. Ousted from a group or territory, young males especially may go far beyond the species' normal orbit, eventually enlarging the range. This species dispersal is common to such diverse creatures as lions, moose, bighorn sheep, and many others, including primates.

The phenomenon is of interest to philosophers and psychologists as well as to biologists, since humans, too, are possessed of an urge to disperse, starting in adolescence when home seems to be the dullest, most annoying place in the universe. Among humans, perhaps the most famous wanderers are the Australian aborigines, who periodically take off on "walkabouts" of many months or more, but Eskimos are equally people who love travel. Without warning, a whole family may decide to visit relatives five hundred miles away and quickly hitch up their dogs or pack their snowmobile and move off, even in a blizzard.

Polar bears occasionally strike out boldly on prodigious journeys, crossing broad patches of frozen ocean. In 1979, Thor Larsen and a crew from the Norwegian Polar Institute, working from an ice station floating off the northeast corner of Greenland in late April and early May, outfitted four bears with radio collars that transmitted impulses to a satellite. After a month, one bear had traveled east to Spitzbergen; another with two cubs got to Franz Josef Land, some six hundred miles away; one stayed in the area; and the other moved south. From there on, their course could no longer be traced because the transmitter stopped functioning.

Larsen observed that some of the bears moved twenty-five miles a day, not counting the westward drift of the polar pack. He believes there may be considerable bear traffic between Spitzbergen and east Greenland. Formerly it was thought that the two hundred to six hundred miles between the two places was a barrier to migration, but aerial surveys have shown tracks between the two lands to be rather abundant.

Polar bears appear to move between Russia and Alaska with the drifting pack ice. From Wrangel Island the drift is southeast to Alaska, north up the coast, and back again to Wrangel. Some bears get as far east as Point Barrow before being swept back again by the prevailing clockwise current of the Arctic Basin. Others perhaps ride the pack ice of the complete arctic gyre, winding up on the other side of the world in the Canadian archipelago.

In the winter of 1978, a pregnant bear made front-page news when she wandered west from Alaska, where she had been fitted with a transmitter, on her way to Wrangel Island. Soviet authorities—with rare humor—maintained she was

homesick. "We shall certainly help our American colleagues in search of the coura-
geous traveler," said Soviet official Savva Uspenski, promising "a warm reception
to this transgressor of state borders. Maybe she was born in our territories and
crossed two continents to give life to her children in the place of her own birth."

4

The Land
of Arktos

Incredibly far as some bears may roam, none can survive for long away from the ice of the ocean. It is their hunting platform, their home of sweet content. Away from it, they are restless and nervous.

It is appropriate that the word arctic comes from *arktos*, the Greek name for bear, for this is a land where Ursa Major, the Great Bear or the Big Dipper, shines down from the zenith of the northern sky.

The arctic is a beautiful, haunting land. The skies are often intensely blue, the snow so white that the horizon is a firm line that separates ice and sky as if a child had drawn it. At sunset, a shaft of brilliant ruby may shoot straight up, piercing the deep blue with unaccountable brilliance. There is something unreal about the arctic, too, especially in winter. You can sit for hour after hour surrounded by nothing but ice and snow until you are certain that you, alone, are the only living thing. Suddenly a white fox is there, close up, looking at you out of coal-black eyes. You feel you are dreaming, that you must shake your head to clear your brain, if not your eyesight. An instant later the fox is gone, and you wonder if what you saw was a phantom, as it might have been except for the evidence of a set of dainty tracks.

The arctic is dreamlike and supernatural, as one explorer, Elisha Kent Kane, wrote a century ago, "a landscape such as Milton or Dante might imagine— inorganic, desolate, mysterious." Its beauty moved that man of action, Robert Peary, to write of a moonlit arctic night: "The great dark dome of the heavens seems far, far away. The stars twinkle with a clearness that pierces everything. There is a stillness, too—a great, wonderful silence. The aurora with its ever-changing shape and color is a constant feast."

Where there are trees, they are often flagged by the wind, their branches on one side only, like pennants flying in a stiff breeze. Very little snow falls, but winds unimpeded by trees or other obstructions keep whipping it up, giving the illusion of frequent blizzards.

The word *arctic* as a geographic term is imprecise but means in general any area in the far north without trees and characterized by permafrost and cold. The term *subarctic* refers to the forested regions at the arctic's lower edge, while high arctic refers to the extreme northern reaches, a place that the early Vikings believed was a dark, freezing hell of snow and ice at the end of the world.

People in the Middle Ages (including the cartographer, Gerardus Mercator, who gave us his famous map projection) thought the arctic was a giant continent laced with four rivers all streaming southward. Even as late as the 1800s, most scientists believed that the North Pole was surrounded by land deeply covered with ice; some explorers professed having seen it. But in 1893, a Norwegian explorer, biologist and statesman, Fridtjof Nansen, set out in a little ship called the *Fram*, which drifted across the vast frozen ocean from the New Siberian Islands of Russia to arrive three years later in the Greenland Sea. There was no land at the Pole, Nansen reported, but a deep ocean with a cover of drifting ice.

The land of the polar bear is therefore not land but water and ice, a giant ocean ranking fourth in size after the Pacific, the Atlantic and the Indian, and five times larger than the next in line, the Mediterranean. The Arctic Ocean is generally shallow, but with two deep basins, one north of Alaska and Canada, and the other north of Europe, Russia, and Greenland. The question of whether there might be intervening land was settled dramatically in August 1958 by the voyage of the nuclear-powered submarine, the U.S.S. *Nautilus*, which journeyed under the ice from Point Barrow to the Greenland Sea in ninety-six hours, with a salute en route as it passed under the ice of the North Pole. A layer of ice from one to ten feet thick thus unites three of the world's six continents, making it theoretically possible for polar bears to circle the globe with only an occasional swim.

Winds keep the polar ice pack in almost constant motion in a giant clockwise spiral, but the movement is complicated by intervening land masses as well as tides, currents generated by temperature differences in the water, and difference in water density.

The Norwegian explorer Nansen, mentioned above, was among the first to make a comprehensive study of ice movements. He reported seeing dark brown mud on the pack ice not far from the North Pole; it appeared to be dust from Siberia, plus considerable humus with microscopic algae. He concluded, rightly, that the polar current had carried ice from Siberia past the Pole to the Greenland Sea. There have been other proofs of the amazing polar current. Parts of the ship *Jeanette*, caught in the pack ice off Wrangel Island in 1879, wound up three years later on the drift ice of southern Greenland, thousands of miles away!

In some places ice may travel as much as fifty miles a day. On the treeless beaches of Alaska you see evidence of that ice drift: driftwood, some of it big trees and roots that have come churning down the Mackenzie River during floods and then are swept westward. On the Eurasian side of the arctic, the main surface current is toward the North Pole, moving slowly but accelerating when it exits south, to become the East Greenland Current. In late spring, the ice moves westward past the Canadian islands and Alaska, at a fairly steady rate of about a mile an hour, but much more slowly in winter.

This constant ice drift means that a polar bear, in order to remain in a favorite area, must compensate for the drift by traveling rather steadily in the opposite direction. With land seldom in sight, the cues must be something other than visual.

Since ice is the home of the polar bear for at least nine months—and in much of the high arctic, for the entire year—let's have a look first at how it forms. On still water, a thin layer of fresh water forms and freezes at about 29°F into small crystals of *frazil ice,* that give the water a kind of oily look. Waves crush the crystals into a thick, soupy layer of *grease ice.* Then snow and slush freeze together with grease ice, to form clumps of *pancake ice* that collide with one another, forming a raised rim around the edges—a pretty sight, reminiscent of a giant pond of water lily pads.

When freezing is rapid, brine gets trapped; but the salt slowly melts its way down through the ice, so that ice a year or more old is almost free of it. Early arctic explorers knew this, and would replenish their water supply from puddles of water that sometimes formed on old ice. This is also the reason why polar bears can live on the sea ice year round, without going on land for fresh water.

The ice making up a bear's hunting ground may be glassy smooth or mountainous, but in general it consists of three kinds: *landfast ice, pack* or *shear ice,* and finally, the *polar pack.*

Landfast ice—the favorite for birth lairs of seals since it is stable and doesn't move—forms in protected bays along shores, or it might form at sea and be moved into shore by currents and winds, eventually becoming attached. Where water is deep with prevailing offshore winds and currents, the zone of landfast ice is narrow; but in shallow water without much current, the sea freezes right to the bottom. Landfast ice either melts in summer or breaks loose and joins the pack ice drifting out from shore.

Tides, especially along the coastal fjords of Baffin Island, exert mighty forces on landfast ice, grinding it upward and letting it plunge downward until it eventually breaks free. On Brevoort Island a few years ago, I was pulling a seal behind me on what I thought was safe, shorefast ice, avoiding the ice farther off that was pockmarked with seal breathing holes. All at once, a giant block dislodged from its mooring just ahead of me, thundering down to the open water of ebbing tide. I quickly moved offshore to more stable ice and threaded my way between the open pools. We estimated that a thousand seals were sunning themselves on the landfast ice of a single bay in this area. It seemed incredible that we saw no bears. After a week, we broke up camp and left to search for bears on the pack ice offshore of Brevoort Island. By plane and helicopter, we moved across a remarkable assortment of ice chunks and larger floes, some pieces new and clean, others old and gray. Occasionally they looked like floating griddle cakes; more often, they were tightly jammed together.

Pack ice is the world the polar bears know best, a place of long stretches of open water called leads, of pressure ridges where snow catches in drifts to cover the breathing holes and birth lairs of seals. These pressure ridges, formed by winds and currents, may be massive bluffs that extend, sinuously, for many miles. Below them, the ice may go down as much as a hundred feet.

The Canadian explorer Vilhjalmur Stefansson, tracking a bear in this pack ice, describes the pressure ridges.

> The winter storms had broken the ice badly and it was heaped up in a chaos of hummocks that had the angular outline of very rugged mountains, although the highest peaks were no more than forty or fifty feet. When you get down among such ice, it is almost as if you were in a forest. You can see the neighboring hummocks and the sky above you, but you get no good view of your surroundings. When you climb to the top of even the highest crags of ice, you get a view of the tops of all the other crags, although here and there a little ice valley may open. But the mountains are so much higher than the ice that a man out on the ice can always get a view of them by climbing on a hummock. I accordingly memorized the mountains carefully so that by glancing back at them occasionally and keeping certain peaks in line, I would be able to travel straight out upon the ice in the direction where the bear had disappeared.

To Stefansson and to others, it was incredible to realize that polar bears can keep their bearings in such an icy wilderness.

For four days at Brevoort we crisscrossed the pack ice by air, looking for bears all the way from Cape Dyer to Labrador, and halfway across to Greenland. As we passed over lead-colored stretches of broken ice, we saw dazzling white icebergs, some caught in the drift ice and others floating free. Here was the symbol of the arctic and supposedly the true home of the polar bear.

Icebergs are magnificent inventions of nature that form wherever glaciers abruptly meet the sea. There are beautiful ones along the inside passage to Alaska as well as in parts of the antarctic, but it is here in Davis Strait between Baffin Island and Greenland that they pass—like a parade of ghostly galleons—down what mariners call iceberg alley. One may be Bryce Canyon done in silver. Others may be giant relief maps of the Rockies, with streams and lakes of incredible cobalt blue. Some are pyramids two-hundred, even three-hundred feet high. Still others are towers with wave-eroded grottoes. A few carry big rocks.[7]

Past Brevoort these icebergs move at a rate of about five miles a day but speed up farther south, moving up to ten miles a day with a good wind. We scrutinized every iceberg we flew over for bears, and for three weeks we studied with binoculars every iceberg that moved past camp, but still we saw no bears. Thus we agree with Stirling's assessment that polar bears almost never use icebergs either for hunting or resting.

The polar ice pack, which covers nearly all of the Arctic Ocean, is something of a poverty zone for polar bears, with a few remarkable exceptions. Here and there throughout the polar pack are pools of open water that stay free of ice all winter long, year after year. It is always a surprise to come upon them. After flying over hundreds of miles of ice in midwinter, suddenly you see dark clouds ahead, poised over a forbidding stretch of black water. Explorers used to steer for those clouds, which they called a "water sky," knowing there was open water below. Scientists have given these strange pools the name *polynyas* and are trying to comprehend their cause and meaning. Stirling notes that they may be kept open by wind, tidal action, currents, or a combination of these factors. Polynyas vary in size from an opening no more than sixty to ninety yards across to a giant one called North Water between Ellesmere Island and Greenland that is twice the size of Lake Superior. Polynyas—especially long offshore leads—are of vital importance as spring migration routes for beluga whales in reaching their feeding and calving sites.

Great numbers of seals, especially the subadult ringed seals that are the mainstay of polar bears, use the Cape Bathurst polynya of northern Canada, and, as you might expect, the area is important as a feeding site for bears. Through winter and spring, it's a major feeding area for the 1,500 to 1,800 bears making up the population of the western Canadian arctic. Ringed and bearded seals are also abundant throughout the huge North Water polynya, and consequently a population of some 1,700 bears live on the Canadian side of this vast, steaming, icebound sea. Good numbers of polar bears are found in the Penny Strait, Queens Channel, and Bellot polynyas, and Stirling believes the polynyas next to Lancaster Sound are important feeding areas for bears. In shallow polynyas, polar bears feed extensively on kelp.

Surrounding polynyas are often great numbers of birds, as well as seals and bears, suggesting that the area may produce abundant plankton and other marine life, and perhaps has done so for ages past. At least as far back as four thousand years, Eskimos camped on the rocky shores of a polynya at the mouth of Wager Bay, an arm of Hudson Bay, and, though no Eskimos live there now, they return every year to hunt for polar bears, seals, and caribou and to fish for lake trout, whitefish, and char. Sometimes belugas, walrus, and narwhals get entrapped in small polynyas and are killed by Eskimos and occasionally by polar bears. Greenlanders have come upon as many as a thousand narwhals stranded in a polynya.

Generally the polar pack is relatively smooth and uniform in thickness, since freezing on the bottom is offset by summer thawing of the upper surface. Tides, currents, and winds exert tremendous forces that may open up leads almost anywhere. The Norwegian explorer Ragnar Thoren reports pools not too far from the North Pole, ample in size for submarines to surface. Even this remotest part of the arctic has its polar bears. Admiral Peary saw one a few days before he reached his goal.

The least understood ice formations in the arctic are the gigantic ice islands, up to a hundred miles square and two hundred feet thick, spawned from landfast ice of north Ellesmere Island. One of them, labeled Target-3 or simply T-3, discovered in 1952 floating almost at the North Pole, became the object of a study by scientists who lived and worked on the island. Core samples taken down to fifty feet revealed fifty-eight different layers of silt and vegetation, and rocks as big as ten feet through, pushed seaward by glaciers and deposited on the sea ice. The shelf from which T-3 was detached is ancient; radiocarbon dating suggests it may be anywhere from two thousand to six thousand years old. Studies continued until T-3 got grounded in the shallows north of Alaska, but in 1979 it was moving again, perhaps on its way to the Pole.

There is one other attribute of the arctic that is extraordinary, and that is its silence. One July day, Dan and I set our tents up on a high cliff above an ice-locked bay on Brevoort Island, where hundreds of seals lay sunning. Snowbanks surrounded us on the rocky slopes, and, as the day wore on, tiny streams of water began flowing from them, tinkling across the flat rocks. By late afternoon, the tinkle had changed to a distant roar as thousands of little freshets merged into a cascade down the rocky ravines. Then, as the sun sank below a mountain at midnight, every stream turned silent. And what silence! It was as real an ingredient as rock and ice and sky. A lone snow bunting called; he seemed to shatter the crystalline air. Two glaucous gulls passed over; we could hear the soft beat of their wings. There was no other sound as we lay in our sleeping bags, although sometime during the night a wolf stopped to look us over, as we could tell by his tracks in the morning.

The land of arktos, home of the polar bear, is an amazing land even when you don't find him at home.

Staying Alive in an Arctic Winter

Dan and I were returning one winter afternoon from the first observation tower east of Churchill when our pickup broke through the ice of a stream. For half an hour we shoveled snow, chopped ice, and wrestled tire chains. It was dusk when we finally succeeded in getting our vehicle out. As we were resting, a snowdrift silently erupted and a polar bear emerged, shook himself and rose to his hind legs to peer at us. Only a stone's throw away, he had lain beneath the snow all the time we were working, and now he started walking towards us. We grabbed the rifle from the back of the pickup, jumped inside and started off. Much as we wanted to study and photograph him, we could ill afford to be stuck again and risk spending the night in the dubious safety of the pickup's cab.

The bear, reluctant to leave the comfort of his subniveous bed, was obeying the first law of survival for both man and beast in the arctic: get down out of the wind. Cold without wind is strangely gentle; one feels little, almost no discomfort. The body seems encased in a cocoon of warmth. But wind slashes at the skin with penknives; eyes water; eyelids freeze to the cheeks. At 25° below zero with thirty-mile-an-hour winds, human noses and cheeks freeze white in thirty seconds. Prudent travelers stop, build an igloo or pitch a tent, and wait out the storm in comfort. Sled dogs curl up, back to the wind, and let the snow fill their guard hairs with an insulating blanket.

All arctic animals are remarkably at home in winter. We watched a little cub we called Spunky walk directly into that fierce wind, head lifted, little black nose sniffing a scent that commanded her to come. As she walked across a frozen lake beside us, she seemed unconscious of the blizzard. She was heading for a particular drift where she dug down out of the wind with what seemed to be voluptuous pleasure. With a few rakes of her paddle-shaped front feet, she scooped out a depression, then thrust her small head under the crust and collapsed, as dogs sometimes do, at full length.

In the worst of blizzards, the little arctic fox, that phantom of the ice, bounces along happily in a coat that seems several sizes too big. When the fox is asleep with its head hidden by fur, it is hard to tell where the circle begins and ends. When I called to one, a black nose lifted and two charcoal eyes looked up sleepily. When it lowered its head again, there was nothing but an unbroken fur muff.

23

Animals in the arctic have several common characteristics that aid them in surviving their environment, most noticeably their whiteness. Polar bears, foxes, arctic hares (in the far north), snowy owls, and some gyrfalcons are white the year round; others, among them weasels, ptarmigan, and some lemmings turn white in winter. Most arctic animals are bigger and have shorter limbs than their southern counterparts. This tendency for completely unrelated animals to develop common characteristics when challenged by the climate is what scientists call *convergent evolution*. A large size is an advantage in this cold land; a high percentage of body mass compared to external surface is heat conservative. Arctic hares are bigger than their southern relatives; so too are wolves. Most arctic animals have relatively short, furry ears, suffused with a heavy network of blood vessels that keep them warm.

But other adaptations to the cold are unique to a species. Some fish actually have antifreeze in their veins: Certain kinds of seals have flippers with veins and arteries that touch each other, speeding up blood flow and keeping the flippers warm. Snowy owls delegate hatching responsibilities to their oldest chicks, permitting both parents to forage while the eggs are kept warm. Some plants grow their own insulation or complete their life cycle in a very short time; the poppy pushes up, flowers and seeds in fifteen days.

The polar bear is no less remarkable. Strangely, his fur is shorter and less dense than that of other North American bears, seldom over two and a half inches in length except for the long feathering at the back of the legs. In water, the polar bear's fur has no insulating value. Animals more completely aquatic—like beaver and otter—have fur that traps a layer of air next to the skin, but a bear's fur gets thoroughly wet. What keeps the bear from freezing in water is a layer of blubber as much as three and even four inches thick over the rear quarters. The bear's long guard hairs shed water easily; after emerging, bears shake just as dogs do, the water spraying all about them. This water-repellent character is what makes a piece of fur so effective in icing the runners of komatiks, heavy sleds built by the Eskimos for traveling on sea ice. Water clings just long enough to give an even application of ice.

What makes polar bear fur extraordinary is a characteristic recently discovered by researchers when they attempted to make a census of bears using infrared photography, a technique that records differences in temperature on heat-sensitive film, making it possible to differentiate between vegetation, rocks, ground cover, clouds, and many other features. Even from a mile or more high, wild animals show up as small dots of red on heat-sensitive film. Here, thought biologists, would be the ideal device for making censuses of polar bears and of the snow-white baby seals they feed upon. Unfortunately, it turned out that neither bears nor seals had external temperatures much above that of the snow and ice around them, so they made no impression on the film. Yet with ultraviolet light, both seal pups and bears showed up much darker than the background snow and ice. This means that the snow reflected light but the animals didn't. How could that be? Doesn't the color white always reflect heat?

Malcolm Henry, a U.S. Army researcher concerned with arctic equipment and clothing, delved into the puzzle. Using an electron scanning microscope, he found that the hair of polar bears is hollow, with no white pigment, and that the rough inner surfaces reflect visible light and therefore appear white, just as transparent snowflakes appear white. He concluded that each hair is a miniature light pipe that funnels only ultraviolet light down through its core to be absorbed by the black skin. What this means in practical terms is that the polar bear pelt is nearly ideal as a solar heat-convector. The fur produces a greenhouse effect, trapping solar energy where it can be stored with slight losses by conduction, convection, or radiation, and operating independently of solar angle.[8]

But beyond all that, polar bears—as well as black and grizzly bears—are able to hibernate, and this is profoundly important in the feast-or-famine cycle of their year. Bears store their food for hibernation not in underground pantries as squirrels and certain other rodents do, but on their backs and rumps in the form of fat. An adult male polar bear has a stomach capacity of 150 pounds, and this, along with his preference for high-energy blubber, lets him store up vast energy reserves during good hunting.

Bears that are good enough hunters to exercise a preference feed largely on seal blubber, leaving the meat. That preference is important to their survival, not only because of the greater caloric value of blubber but also because when fat breaks down, it yields carbon dioxide and water and nothing else. Protein metabolism, on the other hand, yields many products that require urinary excretion. A mother bear's own fat supply during her long confinement is what supplies her with the liquid she needs for her milk as well as for keeping her body from dehydrating.

Medical researchers are amazed at the hibernation of bears. Ralph A. Nelson, formerly with the Mayo Clinic, now director of research at the Carle Foundation and professor of nutrition at the University of Illinois, is one of several scientists who have been delving into the metabolism of hibernation. He says in a study "Protein and Fat Metabolism in Hibernating Bears":

> In an evolutionary sense, hibernation in the bear represents perhaps the most refined response to starvation of any hibernating or nonhibernating mammal. The bear is considered a hibernator because its reactions are similar to those of small hibernating animals that show a decreased heart rate, metabolic rate, and body temperature. Nevertheless there are several reasons why its hibernation is unique. The bear hibernates at a nearly normal body temperature, 31° to 35°C. Its dormancy is continuous from 3 to 7 months. Although expending about 4,000 kilocalories per day (calculations based on body fat utilization rates), the bear neither eats, drinks, urinates, nor defecates. It is easily aroused into a mobile, reactive state, aware of its surroundings, able to defend itself. Female bears give birth to cubs and nurse them under these stressful conditions. . . . In contrast with small mammals, the adaptation of the bear in winter can be best described with one word, extraordinary.

The arctic ground squirrel hibernates for up to seven months, with body temperatures just above freezing, but the hibernation is intermittent, lasting only three to nine days at a time. The animal wakes up, urinates, perhaps eats and then goes back to sleep, completely at the mercy of predators except for the protection of its underground den. But bears hibernate without the interruptions that seem necessary to the deep hibernators. Combustion of fat alone supplies the bear's sustenance. So far no other animal has been known to keep alive and healthy for months without food or water and with body temperatures near normal. Male black bears, carefully monitored during hibernation, remained alert and active without food or drink, using up no lean body mass; they didn't get anemic, and their weight loss of 15 to 25 percent was strictly fat. "What a way to lose weight," commented P. J. Palumbo of the Mayo Clinic. "Sleep away your fat!"

Deep hibernators such as chipmunks, ground squirrels, woodchucks, and others, pass out completely. A woodchuck's heartbeat rate drops from eighty a minute to barely five, and his temperature to just above freezing. To reach this state of suspended life takes several days, and to rouse himself also takes several days. Safe in a burrow far underground, these hibernators can afford the luxury of deep sleep.

But bears in their shallow dens must be ready for emergencies, and they are, even though their pulse rate drops to eight beats a minute from its normal sleep rate of fifty-three to eighty-five beats. A sleeping bear can come awake in an instant.[9] One black bear lived with our family for several years and spent the winter sleeping in an unheated shed, where temperatures sometimes dropped as low as 30° below zero. Yet no matter how quietly we crept up on her, we never caught her asleep. Sometimes she remained motionless, one eye looking intently at us. Despite her lowered metabolism, her hearing must have remained as acute as ever. When we brought her food, she generally spurned it though she had been ravenous only weeks earlier. We could seldom coax her outside her shed in midwinter, even on warm days, and when she did come out, the feel of snow seemed to pain her. Yet in March, she seemed to love the feel of snow underfoot, galloping through lingering drifts with what amounted to abandon. A myth prevalent from North America to northern Europe and northeastern Siberia holds that bears suck nourishment from their paws during hibernation, and this is the reason for their sore feet. Lynn Rogers, of the University of Minnesota, discovered that black bears do indeed lick their feet during hibernation, because they shed their foot pads over a period of a few days or weeks, often eating the dead skin.

Top medical researchers, fascinated by the hibernation of bears, hope that, by understanding the life processes involved, they can someday apply their knowledge to cure human ailments. Nelson has been studying the blood chemistry of all three species of bears throughout the seasons, correlating changes in blood components with their behavior. He and five others have postulated four biochemical stages a year for black and grizzly bears. Stage 1, from September to March, is *hibernation*, with no intake of food or water, no defecation or urination, and no dehydration or buildup of excess nitrogen in the blood. Stage 2, during April, is a transitional period, what they call *walking hibernation* in which bears are active, but eat and excrete very little. Stage 3, from May to August, is *normal activity*, in which metabolism is like that of nonhibernating animals, including man. Stage 4, during a few weeks of early fall, is a time of great activity and food intake that scientists term *hyperphagia*, where calorie intake comes close to two million a day!

It is interesting to note that in autumn, when blacks and grizzlies are gorging themselves, polar bears around Hudson Bay, at least, are yawning and go hungry; in the spring, when polar bears are feasting on seals, blacks and grizzlies go hungry. The feast-or-famine cycle is exactly reversed. All, however, hibernate, although for different lengths of time. Black bears, fat and sleek from their feast of acorns and beechnuts and chokecherries, move into shallow dens as fall winds start blowing. Grizzlies take to caves under upturned trees or scooped out of gravelly hillsides. Polar bears dig themselves—at least temporarily—into snowdrifts.

Nelson and his cohorts suggest that polar bears are in the stage of walking hibernation from September, all winter long and through March. Besides their blood components, the pattern of their food preferences suggests hibernation.

The fact that a bear stops eating does not induce hibernation. Bears in the wild which die from unknown causes may simply have failed to achieve hibernation. Two laboratory bears that died in winter, says Nelson, emphasize the difference in physiological state between hibernation and starvation. The two bears that died lost 30 percent of their body weight in less than three weeks, more than the amount a bear normally loses in three months of hibernation.

Some mechanism or hormone must induce the hibernation state and there is growing evidence that such a substance does indeed exist.

A substance called 'trigger' in the blood of hibernating ground squirrels, woodchucks, and arctic mammals will induce hibernation in ground squirrels in summer. Urine from hibernating ground squirrels will also induce hibernation in ground squirrels in summer. The substance has been likened to insulin in that it is a substance biologically identical, or nearly so, across phylogenetic lines. In fact, there is evidence that the 'trigger' substance not only crosses phylogenetic lines of different deep hibernators, it crosses over to mammals who do not hibernate.

The body temperature of rats injected with a brain extract from hibernating ground squirrels dropped to 5°C and remained there for one hour and as long as thirty hours.

The possibility that research may discover a "hibernation hormone" is electrifying. It might be used to produce a deep sleep in humans during which an ailing body might heal itself. Such a sleep might sustain life, too, during long periods of famine or even interplanetary travel.

Much further north, at Barrow on the Arctic Ocean, G. Edgar Folk Jr., working with captive male polar bears, at the Naval Arctic Research Laboratory, found that, in the coldest part of winter, bears curled themselves into a tight ball and dozed off. After a week of drowsing, body temperatures fell only 4 or 5 degrees, but the bears' pulse rate dropped drastically, reaching its lowest point— eight to ten beats a minute—around midnight. That diurnal cycle persisted, thanks to some mysterious internal clock, even in midwinter when the sun never shone.

Such midwinter sleep has not been observed at the Churchill Laboratory, perhaps, says Folk, because the weather isn't cold enough. "A bear has to feel pretty miserable before he wants to curl up," says Folk, "and must be fat, too."

All bears make winter dens, but how long they use them is a matter of dispute. Jack Lentfer says that in Alaska only pregnant females go into winter dens for extended periods; his information is based on observations and kill reports of Eskimos. C. Richard Harington, a Canadian researcher, reports that big males and subadults may stay in dens from a day or two up to three or four months, and that nonpregnant females may stay up to six months. Immature bears and females with yearling cubs may den from October to January.

Several biologists believe that bears, except for pregnant females, take refuge in temporary dens only to wait out a blizzard. Most Eskimos, however, disagree. Father Van de Velde has compiled data to show that a large percentage of all male bears taken by Eskimos were in winter igloos. In *Eskimo* he writes:

> Contrary to what we often read, it has been proven that the female is not the only one to take shelter under the snow during the winter. The males, too, at least a certain number of them, also dig their own igloos. However, they leave them more readily as soon as the temperature moderates and seem to abandon them fairly early in February. It is also likely that a certain number of them spend the entire winter in the open, especially when their reserves of fat are insufficient and force them to look for food.

He says that bears rapidly enlarge their dens, even at the beginning of winter, with several communicating rooms. As early as mid-October, Eskimos have discovered both males and females "comfortably ensconced."

My companion, Dan Guravich, and I had no trouble finding the temporary dens—or what Stirling prefers to call sleeping pits—of polar bears out on the ice. One year in November, as we passed along the coast of Hudson Bay by helicopter, five big males erupted out of the drifts, giving us some unique photographs of bears beside their igloos.

Running bears pace, like the legendary Dan Patch, the legs on each side moving in unison, an unusual gait. This old bear will soon stop to cool off.

Faces are a rough clue to age and sex. Slim and unscarred, this face suggests a subadult female.

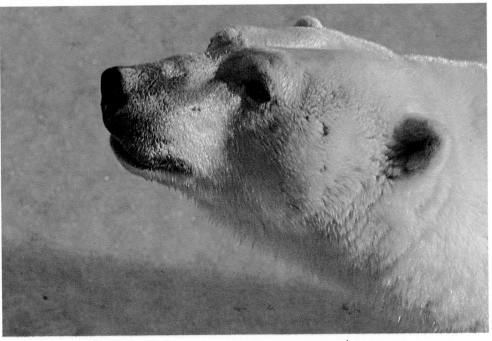

The broader, heavier face of a male, with a little scarring, suggests he is a five-year-old.

A veteran of many a March battle over females, this old male weighed about 1,100 pounds.

All winter bears lead solitary lives out on the ice; but at the southern edge of their range, summer melt forces them ashore where they must wait for freezeup.

RIGHT, TOP:
Their postures are delightfully varied. They may sit like a sphinx or rise on their haunches.

RIGHT, BOTTOM:
They stand with ease and even walk erect for a few steps.

Much of his life is spent in the total darkness of an arctic winter and in the long shadows of dawn and dusk during spring and autumn.

Color varies from golden to blue white. This old male, arthritic and scarred by battle, may live to be thirty. One in the high arctic was thirty-three.

Suddenly the day of freezeup comes and every bear leaves for a winter of hunting seals at the seals' breathing holes. Caught up with excitement, they hurry off.

Bears spend about as much time as humans in sleep, but for much of the year their sleep is deeper.

Medical researchers describe a bear's life in fall and winter as "walking hibernation." A sleep hormone may be responsible.

Heartbeat and respiration drop drastically. Other hibernators den up to sleep, for protection against predators as well as cold.

During the worst blizzards, bears dig into drifts and wait out the storm. As we flew over Foxe Island on Hudson Bay, five heads popped out of the snow.

Five big males emerged from their dens. A bear's day-bed is normally shallow and temporary. Drifting snow probably covered these more deeply.

6

A Rugged
Body

Few animals are more in tune with their environment or are better equipped for it than polar bears. Their eyesight is good, especially for moving objects, less so for stationary ones. Surprisingly in an animal so big, the eyes are smaller than a human's (twenty millimeters compared to twenty-three to twenty-four). The muscles that widen and narrow the pupils are well developed, permitting vision within wide limits of light. Their night vision is better than a human's, because of a layer of tissue behind the retina called the tapetum, which reflects light back to the retina, intensifying it, and causing their eyes to shine when you look for them by flashlight. Their ability to judge distances is excellent, thanks to good binocular vision. David J. Piggins of the University of Guelph, who has studied the eyes of polar bears, says that, unlike otters and other amphibious mammals, polar bears perceive underwater objects no better than a man, evidence perhaps of their relatively recent involvement with the sea.

The polar bear's hearing is excellent, though he might not even flinch when a firecracker explodes beside him. Such sounds are common out on the freezing, cracking, grinding ice pack. His ears also register high-pitched squeaks. Stirling watched a polar bear home in on a vole hidden in the deep grass. The bear turned its head from side to side, moving its ears back and forth to catch the vole's minute sounds. When he pounced, the bear came up with his tiny prey. Don Wooldridge, a Canadian biologist, watched a bear creep up on a patch of willows, pounce, and emerge with a ptarmigan. Whether the bear was led by sight, sound, or smell, Don couldn't tell.

A polar bear's most remarkable gift is his sense of smell. When he discovers a scent, he strikes a surveyor's course. While most other animals circle obstacles when on a trail, the polar bear goes straight through when he comes to a bog or a lake or dense timber. He is following his nose, not his eyes, to avoid losing the scent. A scent in fast-moving air is probably a narrow one like a radio-directional beam. Sometimes when a bear is zeroing in on a scent he moves his head and neck from side to side in a sinuous, snakelike movement that Stefansson likened to the way a railroad flagman swings his lantern on a dark night.

After several weeks in Len Smith's tundra buggy, I am inclined to believe anything I hear about a bear's sense of smell. Often there wasn't a bear in sight, but within ten minutes of the time we started cooking a meal, bears would start streaming in like lumberjacks hurrying out of the woods at the call of the bull cook. As far as I could see with my field glasses, bears would catch the scent and start moving upwind with that deceptively slow-seeming pace which brings them close within a matter of minutes. Sometimes ten or even twenty bears would assemble outside the vehicle.

Ernest Thompson-Seton, the naturalist, was amazed at the polar bear's sense of smell. We know a fox can scent and seek out a covey of quail, perhaps a hundred yards away. A wolf can smell a wounded deer, maybe a quarter of a mile distant. A deer will scent a hunter a mile off down the wind at times, but a polar bear seems actually to scent and locate a feasting chance at a distance of some ten to twenty miles.

A few years back, a man shot a moose south of Churchill, and, upon returning for his kill a couple of days later, he found the carcass largely eaten by a bear. Curious to know how the bear had found it, he backtracked the animal. It had come straight inland from the coast for thirty miles. It is hard to believe that the bear could have scented the fresh kill from that far, but I would certainly not discount the possibility.

There is no disputing a bear's strength. Frank Spence, a husky Chipewyan of Churchill, is a man who, among other things, catches belugas for zoos. He does this by herding them into the shallow water of the river, then leaping onto their backs and wrestling them into submission. A few years ago, after days of strenuous effort he had succeeded in capturing two belugas that were to become the star attraction of a fine new zoo in Minneapolis. That night Frank was in bed while the rest of the crew—and much of the town as well—were celebrating the capture; Frank's brother Bennett happened to stroll down to the dock, to see how the two captive belugas were doing in their holding tank. To his dismay, he saw a polar bear hauling out the second of the two whales. One was already dragged away some fifty feet, and the second was being lifted over the edge of the four-foot wall with a boost from one gigantic paw. Bennett said that the five-hundred-pound bear was carrying away the seven-hundred-pound whale as if it were no bigger than a sardine. A bear's neck muscles are so powerful that he can yank a seal through a hole in the ice so small that the seal's body collapses, the bones broken. (The thick neck muscles make the head look small, and also complicate the job of fitting polar bears with radio transmitters.)

I have watched a bear pull up chunks of ice half the size of a steamer trunk, doing it with ease. (Incidentally, he used left and right paws equally; this one, at least, was ambidextrous.)

There is also no disputing a polar bear's ability to climb and run. He goes up a wall of ice easily and lofts himself onto Len Smith's trailer in a single leap. He moves over pack ice at from twelve to eighteen miles an hour, and his maximum speed on level ground is much faster. He was reliably clocked along the road to the

Churchill airport at thirty-five miles an hour. To Reg Ayotte, a trapper in his eighties, he seems even faster. "Blink twice," says Reg, "and b'jeeze, he's out of sight."

Mitchell Taylor, a biologist who has observed bears from Svalbard to Alaska and even offshore of Russia's Wrangel Island, estimates that thirty-five miles an hour is not unusual and that some bears may go considerably faster. Their top speed, he says, depends on their size, weight, and sex. Fastest of all are subadults of good size but not fat; these are nicknamed "runners" by biologists. Next in speed, Taylor says, are females, followed by two-year-olds, and then yearlings. Big cubs-of-the-year come next, then big males, and finally, very young cubs. Big males don't play out but quickly get overheated from the load of fat and thick hide they carry.

When a bear trots, he actually paces—front and rear legs on each side moving in unison like the famous pacing horse Dan Patch—a smooth, flowing gait.

Polar bears swim, using their front paws as oars, at about six miles an hour, and they can go nonstop for a hundred miles. Underwater they swim with eyes open, nostrils closed and ears flattened to their heads; they can stay submerged for two minutes. Adults commonly dive headfirst into the water, paddling with their front feet until their rear ends go under water, but when stalking, they slide in back feet first.

Seton was impressed with their aquatic abilities and quotes early explorers who found them far out at sea. Samuel Hearne, writing in 1795: "I have frequently seen and killed them near 12 leagues from the land." Edward W. Nelson, father of the U.S. Fish and Wildlife Service, in 1887, in a brochure on Alaska, wrote: "They swim boldly far out to sea and while the *Corwin* lay at anchor off the ice during a heavy gale in August 1881, a bear came swimming off to us in the face of the sleet and wind. He had probably smelled our smoke, and came off to reconnoiter." Seton quotes a Captain F. L. McClintock, who says: "It seems hardly right to call polar bears land animals; they abound here—110 geographical miles from the nearest land, upon very loose, broken-up ice." William Scoresby, in 1820, wrote: "He is found on field ice above 200 miles from shore."

Adults have strong incisors; their cheek teeth are fairly small and more jagged than the brown bear's, attesting, some scientists believe, to an evolutionary change from a diet once omnivorous to a more completely carnivorous one. Besides three pair of incisors, top and bottom, a pair of canines, two pair of molars above and three pair below, a bear has four pairs of premolars, the first three non-functional. All of their teeth looked mighty functional, though, when I sat in a cage surrounded by ten bears who waited in line for the chance to bite or claw their way through the wire mesh.

The color of the polar bear's fur undoubtedly aids in camouflage. There is some dispute over color and whether or not there is a seasonal change. At times, bears seem almost golden yellow; at other times, blue white. Fastidious as the polar bear is about washing himself after every meal, even scouring himself by much rolling in the snow, the yellow color is probably not discoloration. Some believe the color comes from oxidized food stains, yet bears in the high arctic that spend their entire lives on the pack ice are almost equally yellowish. Stirling says he can notice no seasonal change in color.

In their struggle for existence, polar bears are handicapped by a generally heavy infestation with trichinella larvae, in one case as high as 64.4 percent of tissues studied. Most scientists consider seals the main source, but there may be intermediate infection from foxes or walrus or even birds. Taylor believes that bears themselves may be the major source of infection, since they do feed on dead of their own kind. Studies in Greenland of twenty-two kinds of animals show that dogs were most frequently infected (66.5 percent), polar bears next (27.7 percent), while fox, walrus, and seal infection was only minor (from 1 percent to 2 percent).

All bears, but especially polar bears, have a notably slow reproductive rate. Females first begin breeding at age four in the eastern high arctic, and not until five years old in the western arctic and Alaska, giving birth every third year (sooner if the cubs die). In the western arctic, where most females don't breed until age five, Stirling believes that many have no more than two litters in an average lifetime.[10] Ramsay, who has been working with Stirling on reproductive capacity, says that when a male bear is five, the testes make a quantum jump in size. Whether this is brought on by physiological maturation or induced by dominant behavior as a result of an increase in body size and power, Ramsay hasn't concluded. After age five, males begin to win facial scars from an increasing number of bouts over females.

In 1981, Ramsay and Stirling concluded a study that shows that as many as 30 percent of the females in the lower part of Hudson Bay have cubs in alternate years—much more frequently than anywhere else in the arctic. Again without precedent farther north, around 80 percent of yearling bears are already on their own at Hudson Bay and two-year-olds are never seen with their mothers.

In most of the arctic, a mother keeps her cubs for the first and second winter, then mates in the following spring. But in the Hudson Bay area, many mother bears mate in March, when their last year's cubs are still with them; abandoning or chasing them off with the approach of winter when they go into their dens.

Until recently, it was believed that a yearling could not survive the winter on his own, partly because he hadn't learned the necessary hunting skills and partly because he might not be heavy enough to break through the snow and ice of a seal's lair. Ramsay can't explain why Hudson Bay yearlings survive and those elsewhere do not. Perhaps the ice isn't as thick farther south.

Ramsay discovered yet another difference: In the lower Hudson Bay, polar bear triplets are common—something like 10 percent of births—as opposed to only 3 percent of births at Svalbard. Elsewhere in the arctic, triplets are almost unknown. This may be because of nutritional differences; in the fall of 1981, Ramsay tagged triplet cubs that were still nursing, and these weighed 180 to 210 pounds each, the heaviest triplets ever recorded. That weight is more typical of a yearling than a cub.

Other than these Hudson Bay bears, growth rates for different populations in general don't vary significantly.

Jack Lentfer and his staff in a ten-year study of reproductive success tagged 809 bears, most of them off Point Barrow and Point Hope. The average litter size was 1.63 and the breeding interval was 3.6 years. Average age of first successful breeding was 5.4 years. Older females tended toward larger litter sizes. About half the females with two-year-old cubs bred the same spring, the rest delaying a year or more. One female at age twenty-one was still sexually active, and two eighteen-year-olds had cubs with them, but these ages, Lentfer believes, are probably near maximum breeding age.

Few bears in the wild get beyond age fifteen, but some, especially in James Bay, get into their twenties, and in the spring of 1980, Dennis Andriashek, Stirling's longtime assistant, tagged one at Devon Island that was calculated to be thirty-three. As bears age, there occur fractures of the ribs, ankles and wrists, cheekbones, and lower jaws. Some develop a limp from stiffening joints, and decayed and broken teeth are common in very old animals. Zoo polar bears often live long lives. A female in the London Zoo lived to be thirty-three, and a male there lived in captivity for forty-one years. Milwaukee's Sultana lived to be thirty-four.

A Hunter of
Seals

You would expect animals that hunt nearly all year long to be proficient. But some polar bears are only indifferent hunters. Their prowess depends on how well they were taught as cubs, as well as on their experience. Old bears, with years of practice, are among the most cunning in the world of predators. Few others are as versatile. In an environment where weather and food supply change violently, they need a whole repertoire of hunting techniques.

The fact that any animal can find food out on the arctic's snowdrifted ice seems a marvel, but below the ice grow giant forests of kelp as well as diverse kinds of animal life. On the Beaufort Sea, we watched a young scuba diver emerge from below the ice with starfish, shrimp, and fragile-looking anemones, along with fish. Seals feed on all these; they eat a variety of crustaceans, mollusks, worms and other bottom-dwelling invertebrates as well as fish. A seal's food preferences seem to depend on time of year, depth of water and geographical area. Bearded seals, which may reach one thousand pounds in weight, are mostly bottom feeders and thus keep close to shore in shallow water. Bearded seals are a polar bear's secondary food supply; ringed seals are his mainstay.

Ringed seals are as widespread as ice itself. Wherever there is open water ringed seals may be found, even up to the North Pole. They're the smallest of the seals, seldom getting any bigger than five feet long and two hundred pounds in weight. Their brown, sometimes black fur is patterned with light rings. When the ocean freezes over, most adult ringed seals keep to coastal bays where the ice is stable and doesn't shift with the tide and winds. Young seals and some nonbreeding adults, on the other hand, will range almost anywhere there is open water or where recent cracks in the ice make it possible for them to maintain breathing holes, or *aglus* (ag'loo). Every seal has its own aglu to which it must come for air at intervals of twenty minutes. They keep these holes open by scraping with their foreflippers, which are armed with big, heavy nails almost as big as a bear's claws. (Arctic seals do not use their teeth to scrape away ice as the Weddell seal of the antarctic does.) As the ice grows thicker, the hole becomes a long tube with an opening no more than six inches or so across at the surface, generally covered with a crust of snow. Seals keep their breathing holes open even in ice six feet or more thick. In stable ice, a seal needs no more than half a dozen holes. Occasionally several seals may use the same hole, but this is probably rare; many of their underwater sounds are said to be threats or arguments over breathing holes.

For their breathing holes, adult seals prefer the stable ice of bays and coastlines, usually along cracks that were the last to freeze in fall. Subadults and pups get the leavings: the shifting, unstable ice across the mouths of bays, along tidal cracks near shore, and at the juncture of landfast ice and the drifting pack. Senior seals, who may be up to twenty years old, are seasoned and wise to the ways of predators. Subadults are far easier to catch. Consequently you are most likely to find polar bears in the so-called active zone of ice, where they prey on junior seals.

Seals have strong attachments not only to their breathing holes but to an area, probably returning in successive years. Fortunately for the survival of ringed seals as a species, they are loners. If they gathered in dense clusters the way harp and hooded seals do, they might suffer heavy losses. Unfortunately for all seals, they have both a foul breath that even a human can smell, and a strong body odor that taints the ice when they haul out to rest, giving bears a clue to the most productive places to lie in wait.

In addition to their breathing holes, seals keep larger holes open during winter, ones big enough for them to haul themselves up and out on the ice to rest. Generally, these "haul-out lairs" are on the lee side of pressure ridges and are covered with snow. There are snow-covered birth lairs, too. In each of these, in March and April, a single ten-pound pup is born, covered with white fuzz and known to people of the north as a "white-coat." For several days the pup is unable to swim and is almost completely helpless, although it may dig an extensive system of tunnels under the snow. As it grows older it may swim a short distance to what Eskimos call its training lair, an adjacent hole kept open by the mother anywhere from one to a hundred yards away. After it molts out of its white lanugo, or birth hair, the pup is known as a "silver jar."

In March and April, birth lairs are abundant, especially on shorefast ice. Tom Smith and Ian Stirling searched the ice between Banks and Victoria islands, using a trained black labrador dog named Bug that sniffed out birth lairs as the men followed in a snow machine. Traveling at five miles an hour, Bug found a lair every 3.5 minutes one spring and one every 4.9 minutes the next. That's three lairs to a mile.

The six or seven weeks before seal pups are weaned are a good hunting season for bears. It's an exciting time to watch a mother bear as she moves upwind along a pressure ridge, her tiny cubs beside her, searching for a scent. Suddenly she stiffens, like a bird dog on point, then moves her upraised nose to and fro for a moment and strikes out, head uplifted, altering her course only as the wind veers. Once at the lair, there is no hesitation; she lifts herself up and pounces, as graceful as a fox trying to frighten lemmings out of their burrows. The snow cover may be only a few inches deep or it may be as much as five feet deep. If the bear doesn't break through at once, she pounces again and again, or she might dig her way down. She will

pounce on one after another of the birth lairs, breaking through the crust, succeed-
ing in finding her prey in one out of twenty or thirty tries. After eating the white-
coat, she may wait for the mother seal to return. Every now and then, a birth lair
may be so deeply covered with snow that a bear must do a headstand to get in. It is
a comic sight to see the hind legs of a bear in the air, wriggling and kicking as it
tries to extricate itself. Occasionally, a bear gets stuck in an aglu and dies, according
to some Eskimos.

The halcyon days of white-coats are over in a few weeks, when the young pups
become independent. Now the polar bears must use every hunting skill they have
learned over the years. Their principal technique is still-hunting, in which they lie
in wait beside a snow-covered aglu for an hour or more. Their patience is phenomenal—far greater than that of a cat in waiting for a mouse. To relieve the mo-
notony, they may sit or even stand at times, but they must keep motionless,
soundless, with the lowest possible silhouette. Seals have phenomenal hearing,
especially under water, and their big, myopic-looking eyes quickly detect any
movement of shadows.

Perhaps the environment dictates that Eskimo and polar bear hunt alike; actually Stirling believes that the early Eskimos learned to hunt by watching bears. In
any event, the techniques of man and animal are strikingly similar. On new,
snowless ice, a man will tie a piece of bearskin to his mukluks to muffle his
movements; the bear's foot comes equipped with a heavy coat between the pads.
Man waits by the hour for the seal to come, huddled low; so does the bear. Any
snow covering the seal's breathing hole must not be tampered with, as bright
sunlight at a hole scares them off. Summer hunting, with the snow cover gone,
allows both man and bear to watch for the cluster of bubbles as a seal exhales five
or ten feet below the ice preparatory to surfacing. (Eskimos believe that a seal does
this to test the hole for predators.) The instant the seal appears, both man and
animal strike, one with a spear and the other with a sledge-hammer paw.

Father Van de Velde, the Catholic missionary at Hall Beach, has often watched
that strike.

> When a seal comes up for air, one word can describe the rapidity of the blow:
> lightning! You have no time to see what the bear does. We can assume that he strikes
> first with his strong paw the heap of snow and thin layer of ice that separates him from
> the seal. His snout follows so closely that if the paws didn't break the ice, he would
> smash the seal's snout. Everything cooperates—paws, claws, snout, and teeth—to give
> a blow that is so rapid that the seal has hardly a chance of getting away. This doesn't
> mean, however, that the bear never misses.

Two Eskimos reported watching a bear advance slowly and quietly; he stopped
just above an aglu and began to listen, bending his head this way and that. All of a
sudden he dived, shattering snow and ice. His head disappeared, but his strike was
without success. The thickness of the snow above the hole had probably saved the
seal. The fact that seals are occasionally found with long scratches healed or still
bleeding leads Eskimos to believe that other bears sometimes miss, too.

It appears that bears have no trouble distinguishing white-coats by smell from adult seals. As bears approach a haul-out lair with an adult inside, they move painstakingly, pausing after each step for perhaps fifteen seconds. Once within fifteen feet or so they catapult onto the lair, and though they are often too late, they almost never miss coming down precisely over the breathing hole.

Sometimes my Eskimo friend Ipeelie hunts in the very same way. A biologist he was guiding watched him race forty yards, curl himself into a ball and pounce through a snow cover almost two feet thick, coming out with a seal. A blow with the fist, Ipeelie says, and the skull shatters like an eggshell.

In summer, man and bear take occasionally to a new kind of hunting—the stalk—which requires far greater skill. As snowdrifts shrink away and the sun rises higher, seals come out on the bare ice to bask in the sun and scratch away their winter pelage. For thirty seconds or so the seal lies flat, then lifts itself on its front flippers for seven or eight seconds of looking around. Once again, the hunting techniques of man and bear are strikingly alike.

I followed Ipeelie as he stalked a seal on a frozen fjord off Brevoort Island. We started at a fast walk over the ice, skirting dark patches of snow that meant slush ice over aglus. As we drew near to the seal, we crouched and froze as it raised itself, then moved closer when it lay prone again. Within ten minutes, we were no more than seventy-five yards off. Ipeelie scratched the ice with his boot, and the seal raised itself. One shot finished it immediately. Later in the day, Ipeelie tried again, but the sun had made the ice too noisy, he said, and all the seals within a quarter of a mile slid into their holes at our approach. Sometimes just after we passed a hole, a dark head would emerge not more than a few yards off, staring at us with big round eyes for a couple of seconds, and then submerge. Apparently, ice telegraphs any sounds precisely, and seals have intelligence enough to realize that we had passed and were looking elsewhere.

A bear stalks a resting seal only rarely, but when he does it is a memorable sight. He moves forward behind any hummock or chunk of ice, zigzagging his way; in the open he flattens himself like a rug, neck and snout on the ice, snaking forward propelled by slow pushing with his hind feet, stopping dead when the seal lifts its head. The moment comes when the bear knows he is detected, or perhaps he can no longer restrain himself. In a few giant leaps he is on the seal, swatting it with a paw that may weigh as much as fifty pounds. More often than not, the seal slides down his escape hatch before the bear is within striking distance.

Father Van de Velde further describes the polar bear stalk and kill. A bear can't always hide behind mounds and irregular lumps of ice, he says, but the bear's broad fur-padded paws carry him soundlessly and his body blends remarkably well with his setting, except for the black specks that are his nose and eyes. He slowly approaches within a few steps of the unsuspecting seal, generally a young, inexperienced one. A sudden leap and the seal plunges for his hole, only to be pulled back by five claws. One sweep of the hunter's paw wounds the seal. Now, like a cat with a mouse, the bear may play with his victim until the animal is dead; then the feast begins. When a bear is very hungry, he gulps down the seal, flippers and all, including many of the bones. He chews very little. When the bear isn't ravenous, he chooses more carefully. First he eats the skin and blubber, then opens the body cavity and feeds. When seals are plentiful, carcasses are often barely sampled. Mothers and cubs, on the other hand, nearly always eat the whole seal. After a meal, bears lick themselves clean or wash, where water is available. Foxes and ravens finish the feast.

Stirling has spent many springs and summers at Devon Island, watching bears from a promontory a thousand feet above the ice of Radstock Bay and Gascoyne Inlet. He found that bears preferred still-hunting at a breathing hole, but often made aquatic stalks. One swam, alternately breathing and swimming submerged between holes, for nearly three hundred yards, missing its prey by less than a yard. One big female crawled over the ice through the foot-deep pools of meltwater, threading her way like a rat in a maze, her whole hind-quarters hoisted vertically in the air. Seals weren't alarmed at the white object moving toward them, even when it was close.

All who have watched an aquatic stalk are impressed with a bear's ingenuity. Having spotted a seal from a pressure ridge, he lowers himself hindfeet first into the water without raising a ripple, then swims under water, and sometimes under ice. He has such control that he can surface, breathe, check his course and distance, and submerge time after time.

Ian Stirling's assistant, Dennis Andriashek, once watched a female make an aquatic stalk off Devon Island. At two hundred yards, the bear caught sight of a seal lying on the edge of the ice. She took to the water, following winding channels that at times appeared to take her off course. Sometimes she swam completely submerged; only her eyes and nose were out of the water. Periodically she would stop, lift her head up high for a look, then swim another fifty yards. As she came near, she dived deeply and then surfaced with a surge that lifted her clear out of the water. Since the seal's escape was cut off, it turned back towards a meltwater pool that surrounded a hole. The bear was faster and pounced on the seal, then lay in the water motionless. The bear's cubs, waiting some distance away, rose on their hind feet and peered nervously. Finally, when the mother bit the seal and lifted it off the ice, the cubs bounded over to her. The seal was a pup of about fifty pounds; in twenty minutes it had all but disappeared, and while mother and cubs licked their paws and face clean, a swarm of gulls and jaegers crowded around for tidbits. A day later, the mother made another kill. In some instances, mother bears appear to kill in excess, either for the joy of hunting or to teach their cubs.

Sometimes a bear appears to discard all the rules of hunting. Stirling watched one approach a ringed seal from downwind, walking up to it with nonchalance, seemingly not even interested until he reached a ridge of rough ice fifteen yards off, where he waited, swaying his head from side to side to catch the smell. In three big leaps he was onto the seal, crushing its skull.

Only once has any biologist reported seeing a bear catch a seal in open water. In 1980 in Wager Bay, Don Farnell watched a seal attempting to hurl itself up onto an ice floe. A bear lay flat and motionless in the water, watching intently, stroking closer when the seal submerged, eventually coming close enough to seize it.

Occasionally the polar bear kills musk oxen or caribou. On a Danish expedition to Greenland in 1973, biologists came upon three places where bears had killed musk oxen; at one place they found the bear with the newly killed animal. At another time, though, a biologist saw polar bears walk through herds of musk oxen and caribou without paying them any attention. Sometimes bears take walrus, but this is rare. Explorers have seen bear and walrus in close proximity, paying no attention to one another; others have seen bears shy away from the big bulls.

There is no doubt that bears occasionally take belugas—white whales—stranded among icebergs and unable to return to the ocean. A bear lying in wait on the edge of the ice off Novaya Zemlya quickly rose and struck a beluga on the head when it surfaced. Attacks on beluga are said to be fairly common in the Eurasian arctic; a bear there found a pod of belugas stranded on the ice, stayed nearby, and killed thirteen of them.

When the occasion arises, polar bears will take to fishing. An 18th-century explorer, Captain George Cartwright, saw polar bears scooping salmon out of a river on what is now the northern coast of Labrador, near the present town of Cartwright, with well-worn paths leading inland from the coast to the spawning streams.

But for most of the year anything other than seals is purely incidental in the diet of polar bears. January, which Eskimos of the west arctic call *Avunniviayuk* is the time when dwarf seals bring forth their young, and bears are well fed. February is *Avunnivik*, when other seals produce their little ones, and again, bears are well fed. March is *Amolikkervik*, when the little snowbirds arrive, and seals are even easier to catch. April is *Kriblalikvik*, when the sun melts the snow and it sparkles with brightness, and hunting is still easy. May is *Tigmiyikvik*, when ducks and geese return, and now bears must begin stalking seals across opening ponds of water; June is *Nuertorvik*, when muskrats swim in the river, and bears must hunt on ice far offshore.[11]

A Summer
Ashore

July is *Padlersersivik*, when there is no night. In the high arctic, where the ice never fails, bears continue their seal hunting as before, but farther south, the last pack ice melts and bears are forced ashore. Without ice, seal hunting is over. Now for three months begins a totally different life of scrounging, of patrolling the bottom of bird cliffs for eggs and young that have fallen, of searching sandbars for the eggs of eider ducks.

Summer in the arctic is as beautiful as winter is austere. Summer is one crystalline day that lasts for eight glorious weeks. The sun seems to wander across the sky, a little aimlessly—not at all the way it marches purposefully across the sky farther south. At midnight it rolls lazily along the southern horizon. On the flat, featureless tundra of the western arctic it casts shadows incredibly long. You feel harnessed to the shadows, so that walking is an effort. I have seen caribou cast shadows that stretched to the horizon.

Sunrises and sunsets—only hours apart, depending on season and latitude—seem to last an eternity. On clear days, sunrise glides over the tundra, turning everything to gold and making caribou and polar bear and fox into glowing, neon-lit figures. The light plays strange tricks: icebergs loom up like skyscrapers, floating without foundations above a soft haze.

Knud Rasmussen, the Norwegian explorer, was also taken with the wonder of an arctic summer: "The swamps were full of wading birds building their nests and laying eggs, and all these voices from thousands of birds joined into one great chorus singing that once again the earth lived."

In a land where the summer sun never sets, there seems no need to hurry; life seems wonderfully carefree. But to wildlife, an arctic summer is anything but carefree. Endlessly, that tireless hunter, the jaeger, skims over the tundra, back and forth as methodically as a farmer reaping a field, until it startles a lemming or nesting bird. Ptarmigan feed with the gusto of a flock of chickens. As soon as the chicks pip the shell, the flight feathers of their wings start shooting out, so that they can fly short distances even when the rest of the body is still covered with fluff and they are hardly bigger than bluebirds. The parent birds fly at your face and legs when you approach a covey. I have never seen a polar bear pay any attention to ptarmigan, although it has been reported that they sometimes catch an unwary one.

Ducks are sometimes food for polar bears in summer. Offshore islands in Prudhoe Bay are crowded with nesting eiders, each female nestled in the sand behind a bit of driftwood, her neck outstretched on the sand to escape detection, her eggs surrounded by a frothy mound of eider down. Though foxes are far more likely to raid the nests, polar bears do so occasionally. As soon as the eggs hatch, the young take to the ocean, which, though often thick with ice floes, provides a measure of safety. On the islands in James Bay, the old-squaw and other ducks make up more than half by volume of a bear's diet. A biologist there has seen bears make aquatic stalks of sea ducks in the shallow waters off North Twin.

Some bears, at least, have learned how to dive and swim under ducks on the open sea, catching them from below. David Nasogalvak, a hunter from Sachs Harbour on Banks Island, has seen a bear catch ducks on the water. Another Eskimo who had watched a young male bear diving and surfacing among a flock of eiders later found the bear's stomach to hold the remains of three king eiders. Late in October 1981, my colleague, Dan Guravich, leading a party of bear-watching tourists, observed as a bear lay among the rocks of the coast east of Churchill. An eider duck walked along, pecking at scraps of mussels. When the duck was perhaps ten feet away, the bear lunged and caught the bird before it could lift off.

Whistling swans, which loom up on their nests like white markers on the featureless tundra, would seem to provide eggs that would feed polar bears, but I have heard no reports of such predation, nor any reports of predation of the nests of red-throated and arctic loons, so common along the margins of inland pools.

Bears occasionally kill geese during the molt when they are flightless, easily overtaking them. But hunters have also seen them stalk and kill geese that could fly. Bears are understandably reluctant to give up their catch; Charles Jonkel of the University of Montana, a bear biologist, chased a bear by helicopter, hoping to learn whether the snow goose the bear was holding had died of disease or had been killed. Only after the helicopter hovered just a few feet above it did the bear drop the bird, but he quickly returned to snatch it up, defying the whirling motors and heavy downdraft.

A tantalizing tidbit to bears is the tawny arctic ground squirrel, which watches you from a raised mound of earth beside its hole; every other predator from weasels to jaegers, snowy owls, gyrfalcons, foxes, and men love them, too. Eskimos call these squirrels *sik-sik* from the sound they make. During the few weeks of summer they mate, rear their young, and pack on enough fat to keep themselves alive during nearly eight months of hibernation, when their temperature drops to 34° and their hearts beat only a few times a minute.

Lemmings, too, though barely a mouthful, are food for bears. It is an amusing incongruity to watch an 800-pound bear stalking a two-ounce lemming, when, given the chance, the bear can devour 150 pounds of seal blubber at a sitting. Still, the bears hunt lemmings with great glee, making short rushes in the grass and pouncing, although the lemmings usually evade them.

Berries and grasses, too, are summer food for bears throughout the southern arctic. In some places plant life, though limited in species, is abundant. Arctic plants survive by obeying the same law that governs animals: They lie low.[12] As a result, not a tree and only a few shrubs rise above the horizon. The arctic is a land of the horizontal. Nature seems to have outlawed the perpendicular. Down in the moss, plants grow in a world all their own, a world only inches high, in a microclimate so sheltered that even in a gale hardly a petal stirs. It's a warm world, too. On Brevoort Island the ambient temperature was 40°F early in July, but a thermometer we thrust into the moss registered 62°F. Blueberries flourish in the moss, along with cranberries and lingonberries and glossy black crowberries, all of them fa-vored food of man and bird and bear. Only inches above, the wind sweeps over, freeze-drying everything in its path. Cotton grass, one of the sedges, grows its own insulation to protect its developing seedhead in a ball of cotton; the temperature inside is as much as 20° warmer than that of the surrounding air. Bears like the sedges. They walk along, grazing on them like cows on pasture.

One explorer described "hundreds of polar bears" on St. Paul, St. Matthew, and Hall islands in the Bering Sea in August of 1881, "all eating grass and roots, digging or browsing, or else heavily sleeping on the hillsides. Their manner of browsing is very similar to the action of a hog engaged in grazing." Their good condition made him believe the bears had found nutritious food on the barren slopes.

Exactly how much nutrition bears get from grasses and berries is difficult to estimate. Polar bears don't appear to be as methodical about harvesting berries as black bears are. It seems likely that the total calorie intake is small. Polar bears are drawing on their fat reserves.

Snow falls periodically during the arctic summer, but the furious activity of birds and most animals only quickens. A least weasel races past with a mouse in her mouth. Caribou mothers and their calves stroll by.[13] The calves, born early in June weighing a dozen pounds, double their weight in only ten days. Fortunately for them, the polar bears usually haven't yet moved in from the ice in early June, although calves can run almost as fast as their mothers only a few hours after birth. A running caribou is a sight to behold; few things in nature are more beautiful. Head and antlers are thrown far back over the shoulders, knees rise high and free like those of a proud stallion. Newly born caribou run with that same majesty. As the midnight sun drops near the horizon, the unblemished green of the tundra, sprinkled with grazing caribou, looks like an English baronial park. Polar bears generally ignore adult caribou, even walking past a whole herd.

The heat of an arctic summer, especially on days when the temperature may leap to 70°F, is hard on bears, coming as they do from their ice-cooled haunts.[14] The big boss males keep to the windswept capes; lesser ones are generally inland. Mothers with cubs go inland to escape the danger from big males, which, in the absence of other food, may prey on cubs. Some females go inland among the sparse conifers of the taiga forests where they occasionally meet up with porcupines. Once we saw a cub with porcupine quills in one foot; we tried to play Androcles to him, but couldn't catch him.

Bears are clearly uncomfortable in the heat. They pant. They sprawl, belly down, on the wet sand, or lie on their sides, legs extended, or on their backs, waving their legs in the air. They dig shallow beds in the cool sand just above high tide or along old inland beaches or eskers. Sometimes their beds are dug into the banks of eskers or of peat hummocks pushed up by the permafrost. Finally, inland along the southwest coast of Hudson Bay, warmest of the polar bear habitats, bears build deep, sometimes elaborate burrows into the peat along inland streams, going back ten to fifteen feet and more, ending at permafrost. Here they sleep in a kind of torpid estivation—cool, untroubled by insects, a splendid adaptation to a season when food is scarce. As their bodies thaw the permafrost or the roof collapses, they simply dig deeper. Year after year the bears will return to these summer dens. In some places, long, shallow trenches go up a slope for forty yards, marking den sites that may be ancient ones.

More than that, polar bears have a remarkable built-in cooling device. A Norwegian biologist, Nils Are Øritsland, describes it: Just under the skin is a broad sheet of muscle richly supplied with blood vessels that extends from the shoulder blades on either side of the back to the small of the back. In a big bear this total area of muscle may be as much as five square feet. Along the top edge of each muscle sheet at intervals of an inch or two are large veins—up to one-sixth of an inch in diameter—that feed blood from the body core into the muscle. In warm weather, blood moves out into the broad expanse of muscle where its heat radiates out to the atmosphere, cooling the bear much the way the radiator of a car cools the engine. In cold weather, some kind of internal thermostat decreases blood flow to the sheet of muscle. Øritsland also found that the bare foot pads, supplied by major blood vessels, and claws and sparsely furred dry areas of the snout let off considerable amounts of heat. At an atmospheric temperature around freezing, the fur surface of the torso was 3 to 7 degrees warmer than the air; claws and foot pads were 9 to 18 degrees warmer, and the snout area some 12 to 20 degrees warmer.

At Prudhoe Bay on the northern edge of the continent, we went looking to see how polar bears spend the summer. Late in July, we met up with Angus Gavin, a Scottish biologist who has been monitoring the wildlife in the area since 1968. He took us by helicopter on his final censusing flight along the coast, where several hundred caribou were walking, standing, or swimming to offshore barrier islands. Thousands of old-squaw ducks were gathered in rafts along the island; eider ducks were still on their nests in the sand. We flew over two flocks of snow geese with their half-grown young, as well as a scattering of Canada geese, white-fronted geese, and black brant. Arctic and red-throated loons were also still on their nests, and a dozen families of whistling swans dotted the inland ponds. All this wildlife was within a few minutes of the night-and-day oil exploration activities of Prudhoe Bay, a testimony to the fact that exploitation need not disturb wildlife.

There were no polar bears along the shore. Inland, we looked for them above the broad, braided Sagavanirktok River that empties into Prudhoe Bay. When we set down on the bluff overlooking the river, we found upturned clumps of moss where a grizzly had dug for ground squirrels and on the flight back we passed over several honey-colored grizzlies but no polar bears. Gavin had told us that in summer they rarely came ashore. They have no need to leave the comfort of the pack ice.

August in the arctic is *Kruyuat Tingiviat*, the time when young swans take flight. Bears in the southern arctic, forced ashore when the last ice melts, patrol the shore, sleepy but restless, and yawning. It seems as though the universal summer activity of polar bears is yawning, and since I too am a yawner, each time I respond in kind.

September is *Aliarniarvik*, when bears on Hudson Bay are still strolling the beaches, looking out to sea. The day comes when snow covers the tundra and more birds are gone. Arctic squirrels are underground, deep in sleep. The bears' meager pantry is closed. They have nothing to eat now except a rare fish or seal washed ashore, along with grass and kelp. Bears like kelp and sometimes dive for it. Where it has washed ashore, they like to lie in it. We have often seen groups of two or three bears curled up in the thick dark mounds.

October is *Tugluvik*, when thin ice forms along the shallow parts of the shore. Snow falls and swirls over the tundra, muting the sun. Excitement sweeps over man and bear. Trappers scrape rust from their traps and boil them, checking on their supply of scents and baits. Bears smash into sheds to devour the bait and go into cabins looking for anything else worth eating. But it is to the ocean they return again and again, to look out on the thin sheets of ice that form during rare periods when the wind isn't blowing. Every day at Cape Churchill a procession of sub-adults and mothers with cubs leaves the shelter of the willows a mile or more inland to travel out to test the ice, returning to sleep the rest of the day in the willows.

November comes, the month of *Itartoryuk*, when a white mist fills the igloo as you open the door to the outside. In the morning, the bays are covered with ice that looks like oil, a sullen surface that moves up and down with the tides. Later in the day, winds whip the new ice up into a froth of white chunks that crash against shore. Young bears try the ice periodically, but fall between the chunks. On newly frozen ice they walk gingerly, but they still break through. Few things look more ludicrous than a young bear trying to regain his feet after he has fallen through the ice. He spreads his front legs to their limit, paddling gently with his back legs. If he can boost his body onto the ice, he lies flat as a rug and slides himself forward with a cautious push of one rear paw. When he breaks through again after such pains, you can almost hear him curse under his breath. As soon as he is on firm ice or land, he shakes, and to continue drying, he alternates between pushing himself forward on his face and rolling on his back, feet waving in the air.

The tundra by now is a frozen ocean of turbulent snow, always on the move with the unceasing wind. There are very few smooth stretches. Crests and troughs

His head juts forward like a gargoyle's as he hunts the restless pack ice for the breathing holes of ringed seals, which supply his food nearly all year long.

Bears are tireless swimmers and have been seen hundreds of miles from ice floes or shore. Their dog paddle carries them at a top speed of six miles an hour.

Two males flee our helicopter. The bigger one weighs 1,200 pounds and has scars on rump and side. Black hair covers most scars; sometimes the coal black skin shows.

When pursued by dogs, bears look for high rocks or promontories of ice, where they face their assailants. From a height, they can also scan the ice for seals.

For a few explosive leaps, not many other predators are swifter. We have watched them catch lemmings, a ptarmigan, and an unsuspecting eider duck.

His paws, which may be a foot across, have the traction of sandpaper, but thick hair between the pads muffles the sound—important since ice intensifies any noise.

An uncommon sight—a bear eating a fox. Normally, foxes and ravens follow bears, dining on leftovers. This bear finished the fox in a few minutes.

Despite an appetite for carrion, wood chips, plastic, and axle grease, he is a fastidious eater, and carefully cleans up after every meal.

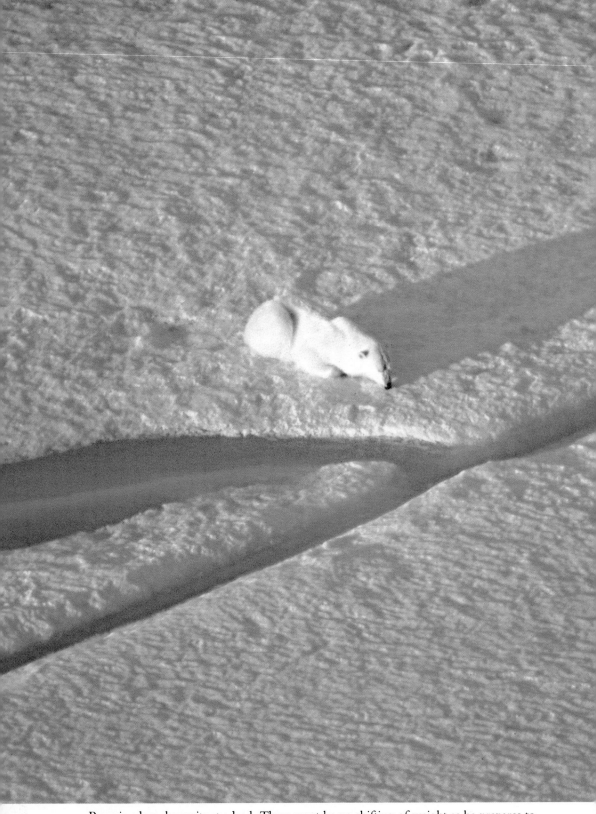

Paws in place, he waits at a lead. There must be no shifting of weight as he prepares to lunge. A seal's foul breath has marked the spot where it will reappear.

of snow are sculptured as hard almost as rock. Here and there are tongues of snow protruding, pointing generally in one direction so that even in a blizzard an experienced hunter need only look to the ground to orient himself. Suddenly, one night the ocean freezes solid and the bears are all gone to sea. The summer ashore is ended.

Life Begins in
a Snowdrift

In October, pregnant females dig their maternity dens, scooping up snow with their broad paws and throwing it backwards out the entrance. Sometimes they find the snow too shallow in one spot, and so begin again. Little snow actually falls in the arctic—there is less than ten inches of precipitation per year—but the snow is in almost constant motion, piling up in drifts along stream banks or in the lee of cliffs. Somewhere in those drifts is where a polar bear's life begins.

But where? The search for maternity dens worldwide has long occupied the attention of polar bear biologists. To safeguard denning areas, you first need to find them. The intrepid Richard Harington, a Canadian biologist, has used trained dogs on leashes, following them across snowy slopes where he suspected there might be dens, probing with a rod or listening at a hole. Alaska offered a two-hundred dollar reward to anyone who could find one. That price, I say from experience, was niggardly.

Early in March 1979, Dan and I set out by rail south of Churchill to search for dens in the Owl River and Fletcher Lake area, where eighty to ninety females are known to den. We would travel by dogsled and komatik east for thirty miles before beginning our search. The engineer slowed the train down to let us off in the midst of a blizzard so intense we could hardly see our way to the baggage car, where we helped the owner of the team unload his sixteen dogs and komatik and all our gear. As we tried buckling the dogs to a tie line, our fingers immediately grew numb. There was nothing to do but seek shelter and wait out the storm.

Luckily, we found snow that was right for an igloo and proceeded to build one, slicing up the blocks and hoisting them into place. A quick thrust of our knife between the blocks turned snow into ice that instantly welded them together. We built the way the polar bear does, with entry below, complete with a sill to entrap the heat. In an hour and a half, we were snug inside. Two small candles lit the inside brilliantly—as light as the brightest summer day. The temperature was at least 20 degrees warmer than outdoors.

In an igloo, as you undress you turn your garments inside out and crawl into your sleeping bag. Overnight the moisture in your clothes freezes and in the morning you simply slap the garments and the frost crystals fall off. It sounds heroic, but it's not that bad.

Each morning our dogs were eager to get started, howling and whining their impatience. Travel by dogsled is not so much transportation as it is a hunting trip with friends. You are Mowgli with a pack of happy wolves sharing in the excitement of caribou tracks. What's coming up beyond the stream marked with willows, or the bigger creek fringed with ancient dwarf spruce? From time to time the leader glances back to you, the master of the pack, looking for directions. You forget for a while that your companions are dogs, until you approach a bush and every male makes a desperate effort to mark it as he is yanked along by the others.

Day after day we searched the banks of lakes and streams for tracks or wisps of vapor emanating from snowbanks. We startled caribou from their beds but saw no other living thing.

When the dogs tired, they would stop for a few minutes. Then at a slight woof from one of them, we'd be off so fast that several times we were pitched over backward into the snow and had to run to catch up. Just walking over the rock-hard crests and troughs is an ordeal, especially in a whiteout, when you can see distant bushes clearly but can't see the ground. You can no more see your feet than if you were in bed and lifted the blanket to look for your toes. Running is dangerous. You slip and fall and are always in danger of spraining an ankle or knee. But run you must to catch the speeding komatik. Our lead dog was a black Eskimo husky that ran in a long, slinking gait like a wolf in pursuit of game. In a land without landmarks of any kind, he had an uncanny sense for finding his way back to camp. Part of the way home he would follow the meandering trail we had made in the morning, but as we got closer to camp he would strike out boldly, taking shortcuts that would save half a mile at a time. Whenever we encountered the trail again his plumed tail would lift, and so would fourteen others. As we neared camp, the whole team would be galvanized; one youngster would yip his excitement.

Still we found no maternity dens. Reluctantly, we moved on back to the railroad, flagged the train, and loaded the dogs back into the baggage car, returning to Churchill.

For the next several days, we engaged a pilot to fly us back and forth across the denning area to look for tracks. Some trappers said we were too late, that the polar bear mothers and cubs were already out on the sea ice. Others said we were too early, that mothers were waiting for the horrendous weather to abate. At the end of a futile month we engaged a helicopter. By then, the bears were indeed on the ice. We saw numerous tracks of mothers and cubs, including one female with triplets. But our pilot, we learned much later, was terrified by bears and refused to follow the tracks.

In the spring of 1981 we finally found several maternity dens; they had been marked by other scientists the previous fall with ribbons dropped into nearby trees. Also that spring Malcolm Ramsay, one of Stirling's graduate students, was able to home in on three denning females that he had outfitted with transmitters in the fall.

Today the major denning areas of the world are thought to be Wrangel Island and Franz Josef Land north of Siberia; Norway's Svalbard; the northeast coast of

Greenland; the northeast and south coasts of Baffin Island; Akpatuk Island in Ungava Bay; and Southampton Island in Hudson Bay, as well as the west coast of Hudson Bay. Dens are also frequent in the Northwest Territories of Canada: in south Ellesmere, the Victoria islands, southern Devon, and the islands of James Bay. Dens on the west coast of Banks Island and in Alaska are widely dispersed.

Bear experts keep count of cub numbers at each site so they can monitor any rise or fall in the population. Aerial surveys are taken after each snowfall during March in Manitoba and Ontario, where dens are concentrated and mother and cubs have to walk through deep snow to reach sea ice. The Fletcher Lake and Owl River country south of Churchill produced 168 cubs from 89 females in 1974. East across the border in Ontario, biologists surveyed the coastline for five years. The yearly number of cubs varied from 33 to 112, with an average of 71 a year, most of them from the area between the Fort Severn and Winisk rivers, inland as far as 70 miles. In the middle of James Bay on Akimiski Island, at about the latitude of Dublin and Amsterdam, are maternity dens, the most southerly ever discovered in the world.

Bears den along river beds in northeast Alaska, and even out on the sea ice. It had long been believed that bears give birth to young in dens in drifting sea ice, since biologists and guides had seen mothers and very small cubs scattered across the ice offshore from Point Barrow, separated from land by considerable open water. Lentfer was the first biologist to verify such offshore denning. On April 2, 1974, he backtracked a mother and a cub a hundred miles offshore to a well-defined den in a snowdrift in the lee of a pressure ridge. According to calculations based on the general western movement of ice, the mother may have denned up in November no more than a dozen miles offshore of Barter Island and been transported on the ice platform for nearly four hundred miles. Ice tends to move offshore of Point Barrow, and this may be the reason so many young cubs and mothers are sighted far out at sea.

Maternity dens are remarkably like the Eskimo igloo, designed to hold heat. There is a tunnel for an entryway, with living quarters at a higher level to trap the warm air inside. Often there is a raised sill at the entrance to further conserve heat. Inside, the dens are surprisingly warm. Harington, sticking a thermometer through the roof of an occupied den, found it to be 14 to 37 degrees warmer than outside. An Eskimo who cut through a deeply buried den on Southampton Island said it was "hot as an oven."

By spring a maternity den may have two or three alcoves off the main area, perhaps built by the cubs as they play or by the mother as she rakes in snow to slake her thirst.

Many dens have a ventilating hole from a few inches to a foot wide. Whether it results from the warmth of the mother's body or is kept open by the bear is not known. At the Milwaukee Zoo in 1921, a polar bear appeared to regulate the den temperature by stuffing straw in the den's opening, even anticipating a storm by packing the hole in advance and opening it up when the weather warmed again.

Father Van de Velde maintains that ventilating holes are made accidentally by mothers as they scratch away the ice coating the den's interior, reducing the insulating value of the snow cover. In some dens covered with as much as eight feet of snow, there are no ventilating holes, Van de Velde says, but almost all of them do show claw marks on the ceiling and walls.

On Russia's Wrangel Island, where dens range in location anywhere from the very edge of the sea to a thousand feet above it, nearly all dens showed that the females had been digging at intervals all winter. One den was thirteen yards long and had five chambers! In widening her chamber, the female had hit a rock wall, which lowered the temperature inside, so she continued digging, each time striking rock, until she finally made a chamber in good snow. Tunnels leading to the outside of dens ranged in size from one to six yards long, each about two feet high. Despite variations, almost all dens had an entry that slanted downward, with a raised threshold at the junction of tunnel and chamber.[15]

For years it was believed by Eskimos that, to keep the den clean, female polar bears stopped up their anal orifice in the fall, since many bears shot in winter were found to have plugs of grass in the anus and no trace of excreta in the den. What usually happens is that bears in fall, with little to eat, feed on grass and sedges. Their fat requires no water for metabolism and there is little waste matter to void. What small amounts of urine and excreta the cubs leave is covered by the snow pulled down from the ceiling. Outside the dens, you see large amounts of excreta within a short distance of the exit hole, where mother and cubs spend several days.

If it is true that only pregnant females den up, as most biologists maintain, then it is all the more remarkable that they do, since their embryo has just begun to develop. Though polar bears mate in April and May, the fertilized eggs—through some mechanism only vaguely understood by science—are held in the uterus for four or five months before they attach to the walls and begin growth. This delayed implantation, characteristic of seals as well as other bears, is a marvelous mechanism. If the blastocyst were to attach itself at once and begin growing, the young would be much too big at birth and would require far too much milk from a mother who lives without food from November to March.

Shortly after the blastocyst embeds itself, another marvelous mechanism takes over as some kind of endocrinal action signals the pregnant bear to begin her search for a maternity den. The cubs are born safely in the den in late November or December. Eskimos have occasionally seen mothers carrying cubs in their mouths late in November, perhaps when winds have blown away the sides or roofs of their dens.

It is a tribute to a mother polar bear's innate skill that she can bring forth two tiny bits of protoplasm, blind and deaf, weighing a pound and a half apiece, covered with no more than a quarter-inch coat of white fur and no layer of insulating fat, and keep them alive and warm when outside their cave the wind may be roaring and the temperature 40° below zero.[16] She curls her warm body around the blind cubs, feeding them from any one of four pectoral nipples. Often she leans against the wall of her cave, like a person sitting up in bed, holding her cubs against her chest. At twenty-six days a cub's ears open and at thirty-three days, its eyes. At about forty-seven days it begins to walk.

Bear's milk—which tastes like codliver oil—is as rich as cream. It is 33 percent fat, far richer than that of other bears. Robert Jenness, a biochemist at the University of Minnesota who has analyzed the milk of wild animals from lion, tiger, and polar bear all the way down to shrews, mice, and bats, notes that only seals and certain whales have milk that is richer in fat.

Little is known of the details of nursing behavior of young polar bear cubs in the wild, but Elizabeth Eertmoed, who studied behavior in the Brookfield Zoo, gives us a graphic image: Shortly before nursing begins, the cubs give a long, rattling growl, sometimes almost inaudible but growing louder as they approach the mother, ears back, crouching, sniffing the ground, then pushing and rubbing against her, pawing her muzzle or neck. The mother keeps her forelegs close together, shutting off the cubs until she is ready. Sometimes she bites a cub gently on the neck, then licks the spot. She sits when they nurse, farther back on her hips than in normal sitting position, her forelegs spread and leaning slightly forward. She closes her eyes, occasionally licking the air with her long black tongue. Often she licks a cub on the top of the head. The cubs nudge the breast from below with a quick gentle push. They suck rapidly, raising both paws, rhythmically squeezing the breast on each side. During the first minute of nursing, the cubs at times make a low gurgling growl. The mother sits during the five minutes that they feed, then lies down to sleep.

Russia is understandably proud of its denning area on Wrangel Island, where 150 to 200 females dig in every year. A favorite spot is the small Drem-Khed massif, a set of huge stair-steps where snow accumulates in great drifts. Animals choose drifts neither too firm nor too soft for their dens, often from last year's unmelted snow. Russians believe the choice of a den site isn't influenced by the warmth of a southern exposure as much as by the depth and quality of snow. Deep, fluffy snow is both good insulation and well ventilated—probably important, they say, while the bear is digging and using a considerable amount of oxygen. Later, when the bear's lethargic sleep comes, her need for oxygen diminishes. In 1968 there were sixty-eight dens here, sometimes only twenty-five feet apart, and a couple of years later there were six dens in an area no more than three-hundred yards square. Three were within four and a half to seven feet apart and two were separated by no more than a foot and a half of snow. This density may be unique in the arctic, though Harington in 1968 found dens only fifty feet apart and Van de Velde in 1971 found a snow mound near Pelly Bay where the chambers of two bears were connected by a tunnel a foot and a half long.

Russian biologists have chronicled denning behavior, observing several females from the time they start digging. For several days, the bears widen and enlarge the den, while mounds of snow increase outside the entryway. A few mothers abandoned their dens after just one visit by researchers, but one remained undisturbed, even though a part of the den's roof had collapsed. The biologists could see the female inside, curled up so that her front and hind legs were touching, her cubs at her head between her paws. In very windy and cold weather, she lay with her back to the den opening, protecting the cubs. The day after she left, they found the remains of a dead cub that was badly gnawed. This cannibalism of dead cubs, common in zoo bears, is probably fairly rare in the wild.

Some females in dens already open on Wrangel Island looked out, saw the researchers, then snorted and hid, pressing into the farthest corner. One female at the entrance, seeing them approach, went inside, came out with her cubs and took them off in the direction of the mountains. After only half a mile, however, she returned by another route; within eighty minutes of the researchers' departure, mother and cubs were all safely back inside their den. Only once did they find that a mother had left her cubs unattended in the den; after an absence of four hours, she returned and led them away.

Motherhood for a polar bear is anything but easy.

Snow

Babies

Few animal babies are more appealing than polar bear cubs.[17] Admiral Peary was captivated: "A white, soft, fluffy thing, hardly larger than a big cat, and instead of a desperate struggle with a savage beast, it was quietly transferred to my arms, where it nestled contentedly, as if they had always been its cradle." He fed the cub from a sponge covered with chamois skin, and after feeding from a bottle, it played with its toes much like a human baby.

Two young Norwegians, Jørn Thomassen and Rasmus Hansson, have made perhaps the most minute study of mother and cub behavior at a denning site on Norway's small island of Kongsøya, in the Svalbard Archipelago. The valley they chose is so packed with dens that one area of 150 by 300 feet had ten dens, or one for every 65 feet square. When you consider the powerful protective instincts of female polar bears, this density is astounding.

During the spring of 1978 the Norwegians observed five families and in 1979 twenty families, studying them from a portable observation hut within two hundred yards of the nearest animals. Of the twenty families, ten emerged from their dens on the same day, a warm one following a blizzard the previous day. Surprisingly, since the ten families were in an area little bigger than a football field, there was no fighting—not even threats—and no female showed any dominance over the others. Often a mother might use a den recently vacated by another. Generally when one family was outside, the nearest families would go inside and stay there. Mothers had an uncanny knack of knowing when to withdraw and when to emerge.

Mothers sat on their rumps to suckle the young, or lay on their backs; they did not nurse with the mother lying on her side. In all cases, the mother was much less active than her cubs. Occasionally, however, she would dig a new den, often near the original one, standing on her hind feet and pouncing to break the snow crust.

Most females broke out of their dens during the first half of March and stayed in the area an average of two weeks, walking about with the cubs and eating only a little moss and grass. At the start, the cubs were unsteady and wobbled as they walked, but their development was rapid. Cubs stayed near their mother on the first few days, but by the end of their two-week stay they engaged in wild fighting with their littermates, as far as a hundred yards from the mother. Much as the cubs fought, the mothers never intervened.

The sea with its promise of food was never more than a few hundred yards away, yet mothers never left their cubs. Since none had eaten for nearly five months, whatever restrained the females from hunting was a powerful curb. It may have been the residual effects of the hibernation "hormone," since laboratory bears don't start eating normal amounts of food for ten days to two weeks after emerging from their dens, even though offered plenty of food.

The day soon comes when mother and cubs start their march to the sea ice. To the Eskimos, *nanuark*, or baby bear, now becomes *atertak*, "he who goes to the sea." At Svalbard, the trip to the sea is a short one, but along the Manitoba or Ontario coast of Hudson Bay, it may be as much as a hundred miles or more, through deep drifts of snow and over a jagged mountain of ice. Such a trip seems a gigantic feat of endurance for a newborn creature. Travel to the sea ice is slow at first, with the bears taking frequent rests. Periodically, the mother gouges the snow with a few fast swipes and settles into the depression as the cubs clamber atop her to warm themselves.

At the sound of a plane overhead, the tiny cubs race to their mother and cower in her shadow, hiding—an action that seems completely instinctive and unlearned. Just what causes the reaction? Perhaps the rumble of the motor suggests the growl of a big male. Adult bears are also agitated by the sound of motors, and big males that pay little attention to rifle or shotgun blasts may quickly move off at the rumble of a starting truck.

Once, as we flew south of Churchill looking for maternity dens, we saw a big bear dodging in and around the stunted spruces, trying to screen herself from the sight and sound of the helicopter. Then—for just an instant—we saw something that made us howl with pleasure. On the bear's back as she loped through the trees were two cubs, clutching at her fur like tiny jockeys. Dan barked orders to the pilot. We hovered, we swerved, we tilted. But by the time Dan's lens had caught the spectacle, one cub had slid off.

A Canadian researcher, George Kolenosky, while flying low over the Ontario coast of Hudson Bay on a survey of maternity dens, spotted a mother with three cubs of about twenty-five pounds each. As the plane approached them, the mother began running, leaving her cubs behind. She glanced back momentarily and saw them, then stopped and waited while they caught up to her. In an instant they were on her back grasping her hair, one on the neck and shoulders, another in the middle and the third on the rump. Immediately she was off running again, all three aboard, as the plane passed over.

After a March snowfall at Churchill, Stirling's assistants Andriashek and Ramsay were tagging females and cubs. Several times as they flew over a mother running in deep snow they saw her stop and let the cubs climb on her back, where they clung with their sharp claws for a while before tumbling off when she resumed running.

When Ramsay began plotting the course of mothers and cubs, he found that the first seven moved in parallel lines, as straight northwest as if their route had been drawn by a ruler, even though they would have reached the bay much more quickly by heading due east. Perhaps they were following their noses, heading directly into the wind, rather than relying on visual clues. The bears moved with considerable speed, too, considering that the cubs were no more than twenty to thirty pounds. Overnight, one mother and cub went three and a half miles.

Even after polar bear families reach the sea ice, the route to a good hunting area may be long and hazardous. Once I took the track of a mother with her newly born triplets until I came to what was, for me, an impenetrable field of giant ice crystals, like the prisms of a giant chandelier that had collapsed. I could go no farther, but the bears had gone on.

Mothers and cubs usually reach the ice with perfect timing; baby seals—white-coats—are everywhere. Mothers pounce on the lairs and haul the white-coats out, gulping them down. After five months without any food, they are ravenous. But the feasting time is a brief one, for the white-coats grow warm fur and start to swim. Now a mother bear must wait at aglus, her cubs beside her, absorbing her lessons of silence and immobility. When they grow fidgety, she communicates her displeasure by voice or gentle cuff.

A baby cub separated from its mother is a forlorn waif. We found one wandering about during tagging operations near Churchill. It was March and he was just out of the den, and for him the world was blindingly bright and unfamiliar. When we caught him and carried him to the helicopter to search by air for his mother and her other cub, he struggled and growled for a few minutes, but soon forgot his hostility and pressed against us, purring in a rough kind of chuckle. The pilot he liked especially and curled about his neck while we searched for the missing mother and her other cub. When we couldn't find her after half an hour, we returned the cub to the spot where we had found him, thinking the mother would shortly return. Two hours later, we flew back, and the cub was gone. We followed his tiny tracks and found that he had stumbled after his mother, climbing in and out of her giant pawprints for half a mile. When we found him moving slowly along her path, we picked him up. He cried with excitement at our reunion and nuzzled each one of us. This time we found the mother and left him with her.

Mothers are fiercely protective of their young, and, though they generally try to keep aloof from other bears, they have been known to battle their lives away to preserve their cubs. Repeatedly, we saw mothers charge large males, chasing them off from the remains of seals, although it is likely that at that point the males had largely completed their meal. At Point Barrow recently, Harry Brower noticed that a mother and cub were patrolling his trap line. To move them away, he dropped a bit of blubber as bait and when the mother was feeding, he scooped up the cub on his snowmobile and raced away, the cub squalling and the mother loping behind for something like ten miles or more.

Explorers, though touched by the mothers' devotion to their cubs, continued to try killing them. An account by William Scoresby tells of sailors in 1820 chasing a mother and cubs across the pack ice of Greenland. When the mother saw that her pursuers were gaining, she alternately pushed her cubs and then seized them and tossed them ahead of her until they escaped. A whaling party in 1868, pursuing a mother and cubs by boat, watched the mother push the cubs onto her back, and on reaching the ice pack, lift each one onto the ice with her teeth, effecting an escape.

In a letter to Seton, Edward W. Nelson describes a mother and yearling cub in the pack ice off Wrangel Island:

> The devotion of the mother was remarkable, and exceeded anything of the kind I ever witnessed. When the cub began to tire, she swam behind it with her forepaws, one on each side of its back, thus shielding it from danger and urging it along. She continued to do this even after a ball had shattered her spine above her hips, and until wounded in various places, and finally disabled.

Mothers are reluctant to leave even dead cubs. Once I flew over a mother and two small cubs, one dead; the tundra around was packed down as if she had been there for several days. I flew low for several close looks; at each pass the cub ran off but the mother never left her dead cub.

With many animals, getting a mother to adopt young is extremely difficult. But among bears it has been done. In Michigan, a black bear took four orphans and raised two of them. Grizzly cubs at the McNeil River sanctuary in Alaska often switched mothers during the salmon run, when mothers were abundant and under considerable stress. Three females, each with three cubs, changed litters almost every day. One female tried to stop her cubs from leaving with another family group, grasping one cub in her mouth and throwing it down a hill. Later, females appeared to accept litter mixing as normal, and it continued to the end of the season. Each female was seen with anywhere from one to six cubs at a time, and one mother was seen nursing six cubs.

Lentfer arranged a successful polar bear adoption. Eskimos killed a she-bear in April 1975, and took her small cub home with them. Ten days later, Lentfer took the cub out on the sea ice to a mother he had tranquilized. He rubbed his mittens over the bear's own single cub and the orphan, attempting to mix the scents. The two cubs were about the same size and showed no antagonism to one another. The orphan immediately began nursing. The female showed no hostility towards the orphan and, when Lentfer passed over them later by plane, both cubs huddled beneath the mother. Two weeks later he saw them again, and both cubs were doing nicely.

The Russians, too, have made successful adoptions among polar bears. Biologist S. E. Belikov took two abandoned cubs to a female that had two cubs of her own; he reports the experience in *Behavioral Aspects of the Polar Bear:*

> After she had been tranquilized and was beginning to recover, we introduced the cubs one at a time. The sow accepted them as if they were her own. She smelled and licked her foster children and soon the four cubs were suckling. We did not observe any differences between her own or her foster young. She fed them either lying on the

ground or standing, and hardly paid any attention to us. The next day we brought her some deer, fox, and walrus meat. The bear family left for the ice two days later.

Out on the sea ice, the young cubs begin training for survival. Stirling has done an exhaustive study of the hunting ability of cubs in the high arctic. Spring cubs do little more than watch, keeping close to their mothers. Yearlings range farther off but stop walking when their mother does; if they happen to be near an aglu at the time, they hunt on their own. Two-year-olds range a mile or even more away from the mother, and find their own aglus. Later in the year, when the ice is free of snow, they are surprisingly successful, killing seals almost as often as adults do, even though they spend only a fraction of their time hunting (7 percent of their time compared with 41 percent of an adult's time). But as long as aglus and lairs are snow-covered, cubs, including two-year-olds, do little hunting. With their mother around, they don't need to. More than that, they're not heavy enough to smash through the heavy snow crust above a birth lair or a haul-out lair. Males weighing up to half a ton must pounce on the crust several times, even digging as well, before they can break through it. Actually, spring hunting (even for white-coats) requires hunting skills that come only from experience. Smelling a seal in its lair is one thing, but knowing at exactly what time to act—when the seal will come up for air—is another. Stirling has seen adults pause for varying lengths of time, then catapult themselves five to fifteen yards and smash through the snow crust with their forefeet, all in one lightning motion. Many seals got away, but each entry was precisely over the breathing hole. Such proficiency can come only from long practice.

Finally, cubs must learn patience, a habit rare in any young. Females with cubs averaged half an hour of lying in wait at an aglu; adult males, unencumbered by impatient offspring, averaged more than an hour.

A bear orphaned in its first year has no chance of surviving the winter. We found such an orphan in the fall of 1979 at the garbage dump at Churchill. It was just before freeze-up and winds were whipping across the tossing waters of Hudson Bay, dumping snow on the mountain of refuse as it smoldered and burned intermittently. A dozen bears were at the dump seeking food, with a ring of ravens waiting in the snow behind. As the bears moved through the fire, oblivious of the leaping flames that singed their hair, the scene was something out of Dante's *Inferno*. At the edge of the refuse, we saw a small cub huddled behind a piece of tin. At first we took him to be dead and frozen; then he shivered and looked our way.

Next morning the sun was out, and the little bear, looking for all the world like a big Angora cat, was busy atop a fresh heap of garbage. He was motherless, it was clear, since cubs stick close as a shadow to their mothers, but he was anything but forlorn. Bears ten times his fifty-pound size retreated when he growled, unaware that he had no mother to back up his bluff. We named him Spunky, and for the next ten days we watched him as he wandered about the area like a vagabond tuft of cotton.

Spunky liked to play in a thicket of stunted spruces across the road from the dump, pulling himself forward on his belly, sliding headfirst down a slope, rolling on his back and kicking with obvious pleasure, then falling asleep, one paw covering his nose. His sleep was fitful. After only a few minutes he would sit up again and sniff the wind. Then he'd rise on his hind feet—a full three feet high—for a look around. It was plain that he was searching for his mother.

Each day as we watched Spunky, the temperature dropped. Ice reached farther and farther out from shore. Big bears, restless and impatient to return to seal hunting, patrolled the beach. Young bears tested the new ice daily. The night came when the temperature dropped to 35° below zero. In the morning, the bay was frozen over and all the bears were gone, except for Spunky. We watched him as sleet pelted his face and began caking his fur. What was to become of him?

Conservation officers, we were delighted to learn, had found Spunky a temporary home in the Winnipeg Zoo, to await a call from another zoo. The wait might be a long one. Though females are everywhere welcome, males are little in demand, since they fight and must be kept separate.

Spunky was tranquilized with a shot in the shoulder, crated, and flown out within hours. A couple of days later we phoned the zoo for word of him. Clive Roots, the director, was as smitten with him as we had been. "That little cub is a treasure," he said. "Loves everybody and is already right at home." "By the way," he went on, "she's a female." So Spunky was given the name of Blondie, as more befitting her sex.

Shortly after, a male cub arrived at the zoo, just as a call came from Dublin for a pair of bears. On 13 February the two left by air, arriving in Ireland two days later. Blondie made herself at home at once. For the first time in her life she had a playmate, Ootek, with which to romp and tumble and wrestle. Crowds of beaming spectators flocked to the zoo to watch. The orphan of the Churchill dump became the darling of Dublin.

The zoo director, Terence Murphy, wrote us: "As to the names, we left the male with the Eskimo name Ootek, which was given to it in Winnipeg, but have gone back to the original "Spunky" for the female as it ties in so well with her background, and we see no reason to change it on grounds of sex!"

Bear-to-Bear

Relationships

Polar bears used to be considered lonely nomads, among the most solitary creatures in existence. I wondered about that on my first trip north, when I saw five big males lying in the kelp along shore, their noses all but touching. This concentration is not unusual. Some biologists have seen as many as thirty-six big males gathered on a patch of ground no bigger than a hundred yards square, with no apparent reason for such crowding.

Food, of course, brings bears together. My friend Mikitok Bruce of Coral Harbour has seen fifty-two of them feeding on a bowhead whale at Duke of York Bay across the island from his home. The captain of a whaling ship offshore of Wainwright, Alaska, tells an interesting story. The sea was calm, but he kept hearing a strange rumbling like distant thunder, and it was coming nearer. He summoned his crew from their sleeping bags. He figured the sound might be oncoming walrus, and if so, he wanted all hands ready for the harvest of ivory and dog food. A crew set out with rifles in an umiak but couldn't maneuver over the ice.

When the crew returned, an old Eskimo hunter who had been left behind said, "Once when I was young, I heard a noise like that; it came from polar bears at a dead whale." He listened again. "Yes, this too is polar bears. You can get much meat and many skins if you hurry." He showed the crew how to lay poles on each side of the umiak and slide the craft over the ice. What they came to find, eventually, was a dead whale surrounded on chunks of ice by more bears than any man had ever seen at a time. One big bear burst through the young ice close enough so they could almost have touched him. One stood atop the whale, seemingly asleep. Two cubs lay asleep, their arms around each other. In all there were thirty-five or forty bears.

The nature of seal hunting dictates that bears stay at a considerable distance from each other. The more noise and shadows, the poorer the chances of making a kill. There is good reason why a bear is annoyed with another one that ambles into his hunting domain. For all the time that bears are hunting seals, they are forced to live as loners. But that doesn't mean they don't enjoy the company of others when they are forced ashore by melting ice.

To study bear-to-bear relationships or, as biologists call them, interaction, you first need to recognize animals by sex and age as well as distinguish individuals. For scientific studies, biologists paint bold black numbers on the sides of bears when they are tranquilized for tagging. But after living among bears for a few weeks you learn to distinguish cubs of the current year from yearlings and two-year-olds. Generally by their first fall, cubs run from 80 to 150 pounds in size; by the second year they range from 120 to 250 pounds. It is sometimes hard to distinguish adult females from medium or young males, though, since females grow little after their fourth year and are barely half as big as males. Males reach their maximum weight in their eighth or ninth year and are rangier and more long-legged than females. During the breeding season, males carry themselves tall and proud and are easy to spot at a distance. One biologist likens them to young men strutting about town on a Saturday night.

Gradually you learn to distinguish bears by their faces. A female's face is shorter and rounder, without the massive proportions of the male. There is less hair on a male's muzzle, making it look darker than a female's. Up to age five, a male has relatively few scars from fighting, but after that his face and neck become spotted with black hair, which grows in at the scar site. More than that, some bears are yellower than others. Some are lean and gaunt, others have sagging "garbage bellies," an erroneous term since bears in the high arctic are just as likely to have such a profile.

The first thing you notice about bear interaction is an uneasiness when strange bears meet one another. The smaller one almost always moves downwind, where he can keep track of the other via his keen nose. If he appears to recognize the other by smell, he may approach and greet it, each gently grasping the other's jaws. Size most often seems to determine dominance, except in the water, where even bears have trouble sizing up one another. Stirling watched two swimming bears veer away from one another, until the bigger one apparently changed its estimate and returned to chase the much smaller one off.

Repeatedly, however, bears confound all attempts at generalizing. As Dan and I watched, two bears approached us from different directions moving in that long, deceptive, apparently slow stride that carries them from the horizon to a stone's throw away in what seems like only minutes. One was an adult, the other a two-year-old barely half as big. They met, touched noses, and the smaller one moved downwind of the other in what we know is typical of submissive behavior. There he lay down and waited while the dominant bear searched for food. Later, we tossed out a cup of bacon grease, since such refuse is dangerous to leave inside the tundra buggy. Immediately, there was a roar, but it was the small bear who chased off the bigger one on that occasion and kept him away for the next several hours. So what am I to conclude about size and submissiveness and dominant behavior?

When females with cubs confront big males, the results are almost completely unpredictable. Stirling watched a male approach a female and her cub; at fifty yards she charged and he retreated; again she charged and he retreated. On another occasion, a mother that had fed on a fresh kill for an hour retreated from a male twice her size. Five days later, she made another kill upwind of another male twice her size. When he challenged her, she lowered her head and charged in a clash that left both bleeding. She made another rush, but he did not move; when he returned the charge, she stood firm. After facing one another off for thirty seconds, both bears and the cub began feeding together. Then in typical polar bear fashion, mother and cub moved off to a pool to wash their paws and face, alternately rinsing and licking for some fifteen minutes. A little later, they returned to feed again and the male chased them off. But when *he* went to wash at the pool, the cub approached the carcass; the male tried to stop him from eating but was chased off by the female. Then the three once again ate together. When mother and cub finally moved off and lay down, the cub licked the mother's wounds.

Stirling concludes that males don't necessarily dominate females with cubs. A male could win a fight to the death with a female but would suffer serious wounds himself. The female that deserted her seal without dispute had already fed for a long while and probably wasn't hungry enough to challenge the male.

Cubs around unrelated bears are nervous, generally keeping their mothers in front of them as a shield. One two-year-old we saw at Cape Churchill kept tricking his mother into coming to his rescue. This cub would push in among big bears that were feeding and start whimpering and squawling, thus bringing in his mother, who would chase the others off in a rage. Big bears do sometimes kill and eat cubs, but Stirling believes this is rare, since females and cubs can run much faster than big males.

The first battle between big males that Dan and I witnessed took place just before daybreak. While we were waiting for enough light to take pictures of a big bear, another one approached. Without preliminaries, they both rose to their hind feet and started fighting; in the gray gloom they were giant phantoms. I could feel my heart pounding; we were spectators at a boxing match between undoubted champions. The bears clinched; they lashed out with sudden jabs. Then they fell to the ground and rolled together. After they had disengaged for a moment, they were back on their feet for another round. We were too far off to hear any sounds—it was like watching a match on television with the sound off. One bear turned to run off and it seemed all was over, but suddenly he flashed around and went back to the battle. Their speed in fighting was phenomenal; their powerful, sudden rushes broke down clumps of willows. Dan started snapping pictures in the dim light. We must have been watching this fight for fifteen minutes before we slowly realized that the match was only sparring, and that both bears were enjoying it hugely. We had heard much about the ferocity of polar bears and of battles to the death; it was hard to dislodge this idea and accept that big bears could do mock battle without injury.

In the years since then, Dan and I have watched bears stage mock battles dozens of times at Cape Churchill. The fights are splendid to watch; they seem far more real than the grunting wrestling matches between humans on television. Often for

His equipment for hunting is formidable: strong claws and teeth, and catlike patience. He can draw a seal through a breathing hole with such power that its bones are crushed.

An arctic sunrise turns bears to gold.

Between hunts, he relaxes. To dry himself, he rolls. Bear-watching is engrossing.

OVERLEAF:

Bears sometimes graze as methodically as cows. They especially like kelp, and dive for it in both winter and summer.

Bears seem uncomfortable in wind, and quickly dig themselves into drifts to escape it. Sometimes they simply push themselves forward to get their face out of the wind.

The hollow hair of his coat traps the sun's heat and passes it along to his black skin. A layer of fat as much as four inches thick insulates him in water.

just a few seconds, the fighting becomes real and the bites bring blood, but tempers quickly subside. (I am reminded of young boys who first put on the gloves; their play soon shifts to fighting.) During autumn in years when bears are fat, this ritualized fighting will go on all day between a pair of bears, stopping only when they take time out to rest and slake their thirst with snow. Even in the midst of a blizzard they sometimes fight. At Cape Churchill in the fall of 1980 I watched two big bears rear and grapple as I sat in a cage on the ground a few yards away. Since bears are so powerful, this ritualized fighting may have evolved as a way of preserving animals that definitely have the capacity for destroying one another. Actually it seems odd that more bears aren't critically injured or killed in their true fighting.

Few people have seen true battles between male polar bears, but they do occur, and Stirling has watched them with a telescope from his tower on Devon Island. Generally they happen in April during breeding season, to settle a dispute over a female, who seems totally unconcerned over the outcome. The action is much like the bears' ritualized play, except that there is a fiercer antagonism, observable even half a mile away. There is much boxing, clawing, and biting about the neck and shoulders, where the skin is thick. Stirling has also seen bears with rear wounds, one with a heavy flap of flesh hanging from the rump. Taylor has seen big open wounds on bears' shoulders, muzzle, and back of the neck, and also neck wounds on females where males bite them during copulation.

Although all bears occasionally play, for cubs it is an almost ceaseless activity. They slide down slopes on their bellies, sometimes feet first, sometimes head first. They stalk one another, growl in the fiercest of voices, leap from ambush to roll and bite.

Bill Carrick, whose movie footage has brightened many Walt Disney wildlife films, told me about three female polar bear cubs that his wife raised from the time they were no bigger than raccoons. These cubs delighted themselves with a piece of walrus skin. The moment one took it, the others would turn aggressor and battle over it for hours. Inside their enclosure was a rock, and their favorite game was playing "king of the mountain," one trying to stay atop while the others tried to knock her off. Bill found it hard to judge their emotions, he said, except that when they were annoyed, they extended their upper lip.

Reading a bear's emotions isn't easy. At a distance, especially, they seem as communicative as a bale of cotton. We know more about the black bear's body language, which is varied but precise, much of it for bluff only. A polar bear's threat is probably quite similar. He may approach slowly, or stand stiff-legged with head down, eyes intent on you.

Two bears that meet may move past one another very slowly eyeing one another minutely. This is aggressive behavior. A bear may suddenly see or smell another bear or a human and freeze, quite often with one foot in the air, and remain motionless as a statue. This may be indecision or a threat. Sometimes a bear sits like a sphinx. Or one lies with legs stretched out fore and aft to expose a maximum of belly to the ice in order to cool off. A bear's stand-up stance is never an aggressive threat; it is purely to get a better look at a distant object. A bear that lies down, puts one paw across the other and rests his head on them may be saying, "Don't worry. I'm coming no closer."

Bears are generally silent, but they can communicate by voice. Cubs whimper and purr somewhat like a cat and even growl occasionally, deep in their throat. A mother and two cubs of the year moved toward our tundra buggy straight as an arrow, her nose held high as she followed the lingering smell of our breakfast bacon, her cubs running and stumbling to keep up. Moments later they were beside us, all standing erect, looking up at us with incredibly black eyes. After a while they began to move off, but one cub stopped, turned, and started back. He seemed to have caught a scent worth investigating. He opened his tiny black mouth and began a deep, grumbling kind of sound as he approached us, his head wagging from side to side. He seemed to be asking the others to follow, which they did. He then found some morsel which he devoured, savoring the flavor as he licked the ice. The communication between cub and mother seemed precise; soon the trio left.

Cubs make a variety of noises. When you try holding them to be tagged, they shriek like a cat as they strike out and claw. Or they might squall and wail like a baby. Often they smack their lips explosively (which grizzlies and blacks also do). As long as you try restraining their movements, the cubs fight, but when you cradle them in your arms, they quickly respond to the warmth and settle down. Any sudden movement, though, and they hiss like a steam jet, a sound out of all proportion to their size. They growl, as we have said, and when they are content and warm, their soft breathing sounds like a contented purr.

Big males on rare occasion roar like lions, but, for the most part, they communicate anger with deep, rumbling growls. Adults make a chuffing sound that Christian Wemmer, director of the Smithsonian's Conservation and Research Center at Fort Royal, has studied using captive bears at the Brookfield Zoo. Chuffing is done with the mouth slightly open, with much contracting of the chest and abdomen, usually in response to stress. A male started chuffing for the first time after he was reintroduced to a pen of two females after a six-month isolation, and again during an intense copulatory session. Chuffing sometimes ends up in a continued series of roars. Once, after an hour of chuffing, the male's mouth was frothy. Females, too, chuff to their cubs without any specific response. In the wild, bears in traps chuff, as well as make threats by growling and champing their teeth.

That most intimate of all bear interactions, copulation, comes in March or April, and sometimes as late as July, out on the sea ice. In the animal world it is common that where big differences in size exist between male and female, the male commands a harem, as with elk, bighorn sheep, walrus, and sea lions. But this is apparently not the case with polar bears. A female in estrus marks her trail with frequent stops and before long, she has a male or two following her. Fights between males now are fierce and decisive.

Like other members of the bear and raccoon family, the polar bear has a baculum, or penis bone. (Eskimos prize the walrus baculum—called an *oosik*—which they use to club seals. It looks like an ax handle made of solid ivory.) Eskimos have occasionally killed bears that have a broken baculum, leading to the belief that the polar bear mating is a violent affair. But biologists and zoo-keepers who have observed it say that despite the fighting between males, the act is more leisurely than passionate, and pairs continue to travel together for several days and maybe as long as a week.

One last element of interaction has only recently been identified, and this seems to be the companionship, or even partnership between bears of the same age. During the summer and fall, at least, pairs of bears seem to team up and travel together. On several occasions, it seemed that as many as five big males slept together, digging themselves beds in the snow adjacent to one another. Year after year, it seems that certain males pair off with a preferred play-fighting mate.

Now Mitch Taylor tells us he has seen adult males paired off wherever he has gone: Churchill, the central Beaufort Sea off Prudhoe Bay, Svalbard, and Russia's Franz Josef Land and Wrangel Island. When he tranquilizes one, the other stays nearby. He attributes the behavior to companionship. Though he hasn't seen such partners hunting together, he has frequently found them together at a seal kill, sometimes asleep, sometimes feeding together.

A Finnish biologist describes this behavior in more detail in Chapter 15.

02

How Intelligent Are They?

It is hard to assess the intelligence of a wild animal. Adaptability is said to be an accurate measure, but much of a polar bear's adaptation to its harsh environment comes from the innate features of its remarkable body as well as its responses, both learned and instinctive. Polar bears have been trained for the circus, but the ability to perform set routines is no real measure of brain power. A better one is an animal's capacity to respond to sudden changes in its surroundings. Perhaps the Pharaohs or the early kings could better compare the intelligence of polar bears with that of other household pets. (What fun to have interviewed a Pharaoh on that point!)

I can't help but compare the reactions of polar bears with those of cats and dogs whenever we try to attract them—or chase them off. One big bear had taken a pint jar of bacon drippings from a cabin he had rifled and was busy eating from it. When Dan tried to get his picture, the bear refused to lift his head. It would have been easy to distract a cat or a dog with the series of whistles, barks, and shouts that I tried, but not this bear. Finally he responded when I squeaked like a mouse, but he looked up only once, then returned to licking the bottom of the jar with his long black tongue. Next he tried pouncing on the glass to shatter it, trying half a dozen times before giving up. Only then was he ready for his photograph.

During our three weeks in Len Smith's tundra buggy, we had good reason to try all the repellent noises we had ever heard of. Whenever we made a meal, at least one bear would come. Trappers had told us that pounding two fry pans together would scare bears off. When I opened the door and tried it, one bear immediately ran toward me! Shouting did no good at all. Stamping the floor would oust a bear below the chassis, but only once; honking the horn would also work one time only. Starting the motor and revving the engine was more effective, but with old bears, even that seldom worked. Driving after them chased most of them off, but only a short way, and both Split-Ear and Snaggle-Tooth barely moved. So it seems that a bear's learning speed may be remarkable.

A firecracker shot from a gun to explode above a bear is often effective at driving it off, but this had little effect at the Cape. When bears started climbing the tundra buggy's tires to get inside as we prepared a meal, we finally resorted to using a stick, bopping them lightly on the muzzle. They never dodged. It was something we did reluctantly, since a bear seems to trust you; we felt as if we were striking friends. The bears would back off and sit down, watching us with what we fancied was more disappointment than hurt, as if we had betrayed them. We couldn't tell whether the same bear ever returned to the tires after one blow.

The fact that bears didn't dodge a blow lent credibility to the stories we'd heard of Eskimos killing bears with no more than short knives. Van de Velde says that bears do not dodge an Eskimo's spear. I have no doubt, however, that they would learn to dodge if they survived more than one or two experiences.

Stefansson had respect for a bear's intelligence. "Their unwary approach of a party of men and dogs must not be set down as lack of intelligence," he wrote. "They simply have not the data upon which to reason, for they never before have encountered any dangerous animal upon the ice."

Planes and helicopters are a radical change in the arctic environment, but bears have adapted quickly to them. Most bears fear planes and helicopters, having come to associate them with tranquilizing guns; thus they have learned to conceal themselves from above. Biologists who fly over bears in a helicopter can usually tell whether or not the bear has been tagged. If he looks up, he's a new bear; but if he puts his head down and runs or tries to hide in the ice, he's been tagged. This concealment activity is fascinating to watch. A bear will crouch behind an ice ridge out of view of a helicopter, moving to one side as the craft circles, eyeing it always from a position of concealment. Jonkel has seen them duck their head under water to hide, and has seen them use trees, shrubs and ice as cover when pursued by a helicopter. Several ran into dens and stayed there. Andriashek says that if a helicopter passes over too far or too fast for a shot with the tranquilizing gun—only once—the bear learns to dodge the plane and is expert at it from then on.

Danish biologists have observed the same hiding behavior in Greenland. Bears chased by plane or helicopter crawl into dens and most of them refuse to come out, even when smoke bombs were lobbed in at them. Perhaps this behavior is what makes bears of the Churchill area—forever being chased and tranquilized—so hard to find as you fly over the offshore jumbles of pack ice. Such learning to hide from overhead danger must represent considerable basic intelligence.

Bruemmer believes that polar bears show reasoning ability. He and his friend, John Kroger of upstate New York (a great friend of timber wolves), were photographing bears from a platform attached to the legs of the Cape Churchill tower, a dozen feet above the ground. Suddenly, one bear crawled onto an oil drum and reached up, raking Kroger down the leg just as a bigger one took a swipe at Bruemmer. The men caught the bracing and pulled themselves out of reach. Promptly both bears started jumping at the steel columns, as if trying to shake the men down, continuing to do so intermittently for the next two days and nights. If shaking the men down was the bears' intent, Bruemmer says, it could hardly be instinctive, since few polar bears are familiar with trees. However, black bears and grizzlies sometimes shake trees to get at their prey, so the polar bears' behavior could be an age-old response, going back to the days of their common ancestor. Behaviorists might call the action a displacement activity, or it might simply be pounce behavior elicited by meeting a solid surface that seems to intervene. One year a big female kept shaking the steel beams when I was in the tower. It seemed to me that she was pouncing the way bears pounced at the wire grid of the cage I later sat in.

Polar bears soon adapt to being caught by one foot in snares preparatory to tagging. A polar bear in a snare quickly seems to realize the futility of fighting, and simply lies down and sleeps. Each time Dan and I would make the round of snares and find bears in them, the animals looked as though they were asleep. Is this intelligence or simply the reduced metabolism of walking hibernation? It is hard to say. I was never completely sure that they were actually asleep as we approached in our vehicle. I couldn't help but think of the way nighthawk chicks appear to sleep when you stumble upon a nest. With eyes all but closed they are almost impossible to discern, but when you come close their big oval eyes snap open, completely dissipating the camouflage. Beneath their big lids they watch closely but their programming forbids them to move a muscle. In the absence of further work by scientists, I choose to believe that their closed eyes are a concealment response.

A bear's first response to being snared may be violent.[18] A movie crew filming a National Geographic special was on hand when old Snaggle-Tooth was snared. For a moment he didn't realize he was caught, but when he did he leaped high in the air, more bird than animal, his long yellow body and legs flying high off the ground. His leaps were high and effortless, like those of a soaring ballet dancer. Then he tried rolling to rid himself of the cable. When that failed, he tried pulling, sitting on his rear for maximum traction. Then he circled at the end of his tether, skidding forward on his chest at great speed in a great arc as he pushed with his hind feet. Shortly, he lay down and rested. Whether his energy was spent or he had given up trying, we couldn't be sure.

Whether or not reason is involved in a bear's navigating ability is an intriguing question. Where winds are constantly out of the same quarter, as is true in much of the arctic, the direction of snowdrifts perhaps give the same visual and tactile clues that guide Eskimos when they are caught in a blizzard on the sea ice. Certainly bears with new cubs move unerringly out to sea without any obvious landmarks to guide them. Alaska bears spend much of their lives on drifting ice, yet reach their denning grounds. Lentfer finds their navigating ability remarkable. He says, "If they can navigate on drifting sea ice with no constant reference points, the mechanism for doing so would be most interesting to study."

Polar bears seem well aware of a thirty-mile shortcut across Devon Island following a ravine in the mountains. Bears on Baffin Island have learned to travel inland, rather than along the coast, which is deeply cut by fjords and beset with heavy currents and tides and offshore winds that severely limit the amount of shorefast ice. Stirling, who tagged 231 bears during 1974 to 1979, saw "tracks which indicated that polar bears of all kinds (but most often family groups and subadults) had learned to use passes and ridges to travel on land between bays or other fast ice. They avoided swimming long distances around points or across channels where currents were strong and where drifting ice pans were unstable, or where ice was broken and rafted by high winds.[19]

Whether they see or somehow smell the presence of ice at a distance is hard to say. At breakup time on Svalbard, Mitch Taylor saw 150 bears on an island one day; a few days later, there were only 15. They must have moved from the south across the island to the north edge, swimming the fifteen miles out to the permanent ice pack.

Cubs have been photographed in the water, holding on to the mother's tail as she swims. Bruemmer tells of watching a mother swimming with two cubs about nine months old on her back. When they slipped off, she submerged and came up underneath them.

Eskimos insist that they have seen bears pushing a chunk of ice ahead of them for concealment, something that biologists haven't observed. Eskimos say too that some bears carry seals on their backs. They call such bears *nangmalinilik,* and recognize them by the large greasy spot on their backs. Van de Velde has not seen such bears but he says he has no reason not to believe the Eskimos who report having seen them. He has seen the fat-soaked hides of nangmaliniliks.

For generations, Eskimos have said that polar bears use rocks or blocks of ice to kill walrus, a belief generally discounted by biologists, but H. P. L. Kiliaan of the Canadian Wildlife Service isn't ready to discredit the possibility. "To dismiss this hunting behavior as just another myth would be premature," he writes in the *Yearbook of the Norwegian Polar Institute* for 1974. He was sledging across Sverdrup Inlet on Devon Island with two Grise Ford Eskimos in 1972 when one of them remarked that he had seen a place where a bear had smashed in the roof of an aglu with a piece of ice. The three went immediately to investigate.

The aglu had been dug out to form a small crater. The snow roof was composed of very dense snow and approximately 1 m thick. The breathing hole, which by now had frozen over, was about 0.5 m in diameter. The bear tracks were still very clear and were probably not more than 6 hours old. From the size of the tracks it was estimated that the bear weighed between 100 and 200 kg. She was accompanied by two cubs. A bear of that weight possibly would have difficulty breaking through such a dense snow crust. Lying on the edge of the excavated aglu was a piece of freshwater ice about 80 cm long and weighing about 20 kg. A drag trail which originated 6.5 m away led to the broken open aglu. On examining the point of origin we discovered, partly concealed under the snow, a large piece of freshwater ice weighing several hundred kilograms frozen into the sea ice. We could see that the bear had smashed off the 20 kg piece. The breakage surface, unlike the rest of the ice block and its surroundings, was free of snow. The bear had then rolled the piece of ice to where the aglu was located. By checking the tracks, we made certain that the adult and not the cubs had rolled this piece of ice. A photographic record was made.

What happened next is not certain, but we may consider the following possibilities:

1. The bear used the piece of ice to smash through part of the snow roof. Once the roof was thinner it would be possible for the bear, using its own weight, to break through the rest. Then should the seal surface, the bear would be able to take it by surprise.

2. The bear heard the seal come to the surface and tried to smash it on the head with the piece of ice, in an attempt to stun or kill it.

3. The bear, after his unsuccessful attempt to catch the seal in the conventional way, broke off the piece of ice in "anger," frustration, or play, and rolled it towards the opened aglu, and by sheer coincidence abandoned it there.

He goes on to say that bears in the London Zoo have been seen to throw chunks of ice. Jonkel wrote him that it appeared from tracks in the snow that certain bears were using rocks to set off the triggers at snare sites, and that when all nearby rocks were removed, one or more bears had brought them back from as far as two yards in order to spring the snare.

Jonkel has published a short paper on what appeared to him to have been tool-using. Again, a bear had broken off a piece of ice and used it to break through the ice-covered snow of a seal haul-out hole. He believes that that is what happened, but admits the evidence is circumstantial.[20]

Naturalist Ernest Thompson-Seton didn't discount the possibility of tool-using. He watched two bears at the Edinburgh Zoo. One seized a large bone (the femur of a horse), held it between its paws, threw it at the other bear some ten or twelve feet away, and continued the action for an hour.

03

His Companion,
the Eskimo

Like polar bears, who left the family of brown bears sometime during the shadowy past, a race of people split off from the rest of the human family to go north among the icebergs. Here, around the top of the world, Eskimos have lived for ages with polar bears as their partners, creatures they love and revere as gods even as they also fear them.

It seems a miracle that humans can survive in a land icebound most of the year at temperatures often 70° below zero, where November storms rage at one hundred miles an hour, and there are no trees for shelter or fuel. When the arctic night falls and the sun disappears for seventy-two days, caribou are far inland, and though walrus and seals still swim the open leads, those leads may be dangerously far offshore. Even in daylight, hunting is perilous. Charging walrus puncture the skin kayaks, and whales can upset their larger seacraft, the ten-man, skin-covered umiaks. Fog closes in, thick enough to lean on, and winds blow ice and hunters out to sea. A slip into the water brings death in ten minutes.

Yet Eskimos see nothing heroic about their existence. Twenty years ago, when I spoke to Dan Leavitt, an Eskimo whaler, he told me simply: "We have meat in our cellars, vegetables we get fresh from the caribou stomach, and clams from the walrus stomach." Dan liked all faces of nature. "The spring is fine, birds coming home. In summer, whales and caribou come. In fall we have hunting to do and that is fine, too. But in winter, then we sit around fire and tell story. That is good, too." Such was the outlook of the Eskimo before the advent of bounty-hunting lawyers; Dan was a self-reliant, confident, content man, exultant in the routine of daily living.

Barrow, the biggest Eskimo village in the world, looks out on nearly three thousand miles of ice that extends past the North Pole and around the world to Europe. Outside the village there is nothing but tundra, treeless and flat and melancholy as a Dali landscape; but the people of Barrow were anything but joyless. Half the town was aged ten or less, and the children in their bright parkas would play together along the coast, pausing among cakes of shore ice, then racing on as carefree as a flock of sandpipers. Older boys with spears hurried purposefully down the gravel street. Two little girls on a homemade teeter-totter—like jumping jacks of fur—catapulted one another skyward where they trod the air, then landed expertly with their feet on the board. Children crowded everywhere around without fear, as friendly as their fuzzy puppies.

Eskimos have much to teach the world about human harmony. Sociologists who have searched for the answer to the Eskimo's characteristic tranquility have concluded that it is rooted in their childhood experiences. Children seldom cry. Babies ride in a pack-like *amaut* on their mothers' backs, snug under the parka, all day. As the children grow older, they learn that any adult will look after their needs and comfort them when necessary. For example, I observed a young boy turn to a man who was not his father for help with his trousers after he had relieved himself. Togetherness embraces the whole village, not just a single family. Nor are children reprimanded; many have never in their whole lives known a cross word or a disapproving look.

Dan Leavitt spoke to me about the children. On a trip below the Arctic Circle, what he missed most were not only his own eight dark-eyed sons, but the rest of Barrow's children, too. "You see we like kids. Don't matter whose." Dan's parents had eight boys, too. "Sometimes Father, sometimes Mother took me into igloo all alone and we talk two, t'ree hour 'bout doing good, being brave and thing like that. They never talk bad to us 'bout thing we do. We children like those talks."

An Eskimo's feeling for children may be hard for the white man to comprehend, but after a summer at Barrow my brother and his wife found it almost unbearable to leave little Marie, a five-year-old Eskimo child with a face like an oriental doll framed in white fox fur. Every day Marie brought dainty yellow poppies or other tundra flowers to my brother and his wife, and then would stay to help them make cookies and biscuits and other white man's food. "You love her very much and she love you," Marie's mother said thoughtfully. "You both be happy. You take her." My brother and his wife considered the proposal a long while but decided to decline for the little girl's sake. When Dan Leavitt told me that he had no daughters, I understood when he asked, more than half in earnest, "You give me one?" Eskimo children aren't anyone's property but a gift of happiness on loan. Eskimos frequently give children to couples who have none—not because children mean so little, but because they mean so much.

During July and August, when temperatures reached the forties and above, most Eskimo parents "vacationed" in a tent pitched in the gravel beside their frame house. Dan said, "After you live in three rooms with ten people all winter, you would think it's a vacation, too."

In the evening, adults and children would gather in the community center, don mittens (nobody danced without them), and, to the beat of three or four drums, start a vigorous, stamping dance that might last for hours.

Lay ministers had just arrived at Barrow and one of them built a jail. "Here in Barrow?" Dan Leavitt asked when I told him of it. "I can't believe it." "You don't need one?" I asked. He thought a moment. "Well, sometime a boy get drunk on

Saturday night. I guess we do." Other crusaders were telling Barrow citizens they must form a reservation like those of the Indians.

Barrow people in 1960 also exhibited a gracious generosity to each other and visitors alike. Abe and Marie Burroughs, who had known my brother, immediately gave me rings of jade and a piece of black baleen from a whale's mouth on which Abe had etched a hunting scene. Another of my brother's friends insisted I accept a hunter's trophy: an oosik, or walrus baculum, a solid bone two feet long.

It was summer, and during the exhilarating seventy-two days when the sun never sets, Barrow was astir most of the night, even the toddlers. Offshore, hunters with rifles and harpoons waited on ice floes for seals while others in kayaks threaded the open water, towing their catch home. Long after midnight, children crowded around each returning hunter. Women cut up the seals, each using a crescent-shaped *ulu*, a knife that cuts the hide as if it were strung with zippers. Despite all the action, there was almost no noise. Eskimos seem to speak in whispers. Arctic mammals that have never learned to fear the sight of man often fear his voice.

The sea had proved bountiful. Down the beach, hunters had hauled out a blue whale, using a caterpillar tractor lent by the naval research laboratory. The whale was a black mountain of flesh forty feet long. Women, tucking their long sleeves out of the way, made long swift cuts without a touch of blood or fat soiling their parkas. Each child got a piece of *muktuk*—Eskimo candy: an inch-thick ribbon of black and white, half meat, half gristle, that tastes something like raw bacon. This whale was the sixth brought in that summer. Four had been butchered out on the ice; the ribs of another stood on the beach like the struts of a ship, the backbone three feet high.

Within ten hours, the forty tons of whale meat were carefully stowed underground in freezing chambers hollowed out of the frozen earth along shore, perhaps centuries ago, and in constant use since. Festooned with hoar frost, the caves—each six feet or more square and fifteen feet deep—were hung thick with bright, clean meat of whale, seal, bearded seal, walrus, ducks, caribou, and fish, a year's supply for the family plus a ton and a half of dog food.

A polar bear wandered into town, moving from house to house trying a door or window until he was finally shot. I watched as my friends skinned him. As the limbs and torso were being freed of hide, a form that looked distressingly, disturbingly human emerged, even to the same biceps, triceps, pectorals, rib cage, and long arms and legs and fingers. I began to understand why Eskimos consider the polar bear something far more than trophy, food, and provider of skins.

To Barrow residents as well as to Eskimos elsewhere, the polar bear was a shaman, a being of infinite wisdom, in communication with a spirit world. But even though a god, he still faced the same cold, the same wind, the same stinging, sand-blasting granules of snow. Somewhere out on the ice was a village of spirit bears, the Eskimos believed, and here lived bears who had been killed. I found myself almost believing the myth, so silently do bears sometimes appear. They come out of nowhere and go into nowhere.

Polar bears may have figured in ancient ceremonial rituals. Savva Uspenski, the Russian biologist, has photographed piles of polar bear skulls along the Siberian coast that are several feet high and very old. He has no idea of their origin or meaning.

Until recently, Eskimos treated a bear's body with great respect. Bears, they believed, are so wise that they would never be killed, but only by dying can they get certain equipment they need for the next world. Seals, too, are wise and give their life for a drink of fresh water; a good hunter therefore poured a dipperful of water into the seal's mouth when he brought it ashore. Polar bears had no need for fresh water, but what every male bear would gladly exchange his life for was a crooked knife and a drill; a female bear needed skin scrapers, needle cases, and an *ulu*, or woman's knife. It was important that the bear's soul, or innua, receive those things and be treated with great respect, for four days in the case of a male and five days for a female. So the hide was hung inside the home, along with the bladder, spleen, tongue, and genitals. During the four- or five-day observance, no work of any kind was done. The finest knives, tools, and harpoon heads were placed beside the male skin as gifts, and the choicest sewing equipment and skin scrapers alongside the female skin. In some villages the bear's bladder was thought to house the innua; it was inflated, painted, and hung in the main lodge. During a "bladder feast" it was offered food and water, then later deflated and pushed through a hole in the ice. Although rituals varied with the locale, the dead bear was everywhere treated with deference by the Eskimos. An innua properly treated and furnished with tools of good quality, wrote Stefansson, reports this to the land of the polar bears, and "other bears will be anxious to be killed by so reliable a man." When the vigil ended, children threw the gifts to the floor and competed in picking them up.

Until recently, the Eskimos of tiny King Island in the Bering Strait used to hold an elaborate ceremonial dance to mark the departure of the innua and insure that it would soon return in the body of another bear. A Jesuit priest, Bellarmine Lafortune, who lived on King Island for forty-four years, wrote that after the dance, the bear's skull was taken out on the moving ice, and when the ice made a noise, the innua was thought to have moved on. During one week the parties were almost continuous. The lucky hunters had to produce *kacpadac* (sour greens with seal oil and reindeer tallow) and *alluit* (snow with seal oil and berries) and *tammoagac* (a mixture of reindeer or moose tallow, dry fish, seal oil and water) for the crowd. The priest didn't complain about the dances but asked that his parishioners forego them during Lent; in a year when the best bear hunting came during Lent, his parish paid him the ultimate respect of withholding them until after Easter.

So important were bears to his parishioners that Lafortune kept careful track of the number they killed: In March, 1934, his people took ten in five days; on 16 December 1939, seven in a single day! The dancing never seemed to end. And because the festivities were such fun, a man dressed in a bear skin would sometimes crawl inside an igloo with a loud roar, moving the paws wildly to the momentary terror of the children, then start to dance, to be joined by as many of the villagers as could crowd inside.

Legends about polar bears abound. I have heard a few from older Eskimos; Knud Rasmussen has collected many of them. In the hush of an igloo, by the light of a seal-oil lamp flickering in its stone basin, the legends would go on for hours. Sometimes they would feature the polar bear and another animal, sometimes the polar bear and humans.

One story I heard at several villages, and though it seems like fiction, it may very well have basis in fact. This version is by Yuani Inuppaq.

> A family was once moving toward the sea, followed by a little old woman who could not walk except with a stick; she was not allowed to ride on the sled. She would fall far behind and arrive at camp only when it was nearly dawn. The family was very hungry and chewed on caribou skins. "We too used to do the same," Inuppaq said, "when there was no food."
>
> One moonlit night the old woman was walking with her stick very late at night when a big male bear that had followed her trail caught up with her. Dodging him with the help of her stick, she kept from being bitten. She turned her mittens inside out and put them on the end of her cane. When the bear came again, she jabbed the stick at his mouth where it stuck, killing him. On her arrival mittenless to camp, she greeted her little grandchild. "Since I have killed an animal you will be getting something to eat." When morning came, she guided her son back down the trail. "It's not here, but farther away," she said, "on the other side of the distant hill." They found it, choked with her mittens. From then on she was taken care of and rode on the sled. There was great happiness.

"Stories like this were told when none of us were yet born," said Inuppaq. "In the tent of Iyautilik these listeners have heard it for the first time."

In Alaska you may still hear tales of Kokogiak, a ten-legged polar bear, monster of the ice pack and a portent of death to the hunter who sees it. Few men have ever looked at it and lived to tell, but many have seen a *kinik*, a bear too big to haul himself out onto the ice. Nathaniel Neakok and Raymond Ipalook of Barrow recently saw the head of one that was swimming, but feared shooting it, hiding instead behind a pressure ridge. When it reappeared, they saw that the head alone must have been five feet long and almost as wide. Other hunters say that Kokogiak is four or five times bigger than a normal bear. Nowhere in any of the Eskimo villages around Hudson Bay could I find anyone who knew of Kokogiak, but one old woman, little Granny Rosa Konayok of Repulse Bay, remembered the story of a giant polar bear that lived at the bottom of the sea, and when a whaling captain dropped a depth charge to kill it, the bear almost capsized the ship.

Some legends tell how bears themselves told stories to one another of how they hunted man, whom they called "the one who staggers," since each time he takes a step he almost loses his balance. Dogs, they said, stung like mosquitoes and their barking was laughter.

Being eaten by a bear was not considered the worst fate. Eskimos believe that when an old person was left alone in an igloo to die, a bear would come to eat the body, and when the bear was killed and eaten, the spirit of the old person would be rekindled and live afresh.

Across the top of the world in Norway, too, there are legends. In "The Cat of Dovre," a hunter was taking a big white bear to the king of Denmark when he stopped at a cottage in Dovre on Christmas Eve, asking for shelter. The cottager declined, saying that so many trolls came every Christmas Eve that he and his family were forced to move out for the night. The hunter persisted. The closet was good enough for him, he said, and his bear could sleep under the stove. And so, after a big meal of cream porridge, sausages, and *lutefisk*, they all went to sleep. When the trolls came, they mistook the bear for a cat and barely escaped with their lives. Since then, the trolls have never bothered the cottage at Dovre.

In "East of the Sun and West of the Moon," a classic fairy tale, a great white bear came to a peasant's cottage and begged for the family's fairest daughter, promising in return great riches. The bear was actually a handsome prince who had been bewitched. Each night when he lay with the peasant's daughter he took the form of a man, but by day he took the form of a bear. After much trouble and travel, the couple found happiness when the bear returned permanently to human form.

Eskimos, like the polar bears, are great travelers, moving from one place to the next, depending on the hunting, or just visiting friends and relatives sometimes several hundred miles away. Until thirty years ago, when they began collecting into villages where the Canadian government could care for them more easily during periods of famine and disease, they were nomads, scattered along the coast.

Today, few Eskimo villages are without television sets, snow machines, and even dial telephones. It is doubtful that respect for a bear's innua persists in many places. And yet, when a McGill University professor, George Wenzel, accompanied Eskimo friends on bear hunts in the east Baffin area in 1979, he found that almost every hunter warned him not to ridicule or belittle a bear or make jokes about it because to do so would bring bad luck. Bears, the hunters kept telling him, were fully as smart as humans.

One time Wenzel forgot and commented out loud that a bear was foolish in not starting to run until the snow machines were close. Two Eskimos, one in his middle twenties and the other about thirty-five, stopped work and advised him not to speak that way. Then they turned back to skinning the bear. Wenzel says, "Two days later, at Resolute Bay where I was drinking tea with several families, the chief mentioned that he had overheard my words on the ice. He said he thought that I knew better, but since I was a white man it would probably not have any serious effect."

Dan and I searched for a place where Eskimos still clung to their old beliefs about bears. We were in the eastern arctic on Brevoort Island when we heard about the tiny settlement of Eskimos on Allen Island. Pilots sometimes have trouble finding the island, since it is no more than a cluster of unpainted shacks that squat uneasily on a slender sandbar jutting out into a narrow fjord. No more than forty people, including children, live there. Two or three of the men work at oil-drilling camps on the coast, transported back and forth by light plane or helicopter. A few work at Frobisher Bay, an hour away by air. But for the most part, the people on Allen Island live as their ancestors did, by hunting and fishing and trapping.

Ipeelie Inookie is one of them. He attended high school at Frobisher Bay and was married at nineteen, but then his wife died, leaving him a little daughter who lives with his girl friend. Ipeelie has been asked to teach courses in survival at Frobisher Bay but he can't abide the noise of traffic and blaring television sets in the little village.

Since Ipeelie speaks English, he sometimes guides visiting naturalists, showing them—as he did us—the fabulous arctic flora of the moss-encrusted mountains and the animal life of the frozen bays. It was evident that he loved his arctic homeland from the manner in which he knelt beside mosslike patches of bell heather, which was beginning to open its delicate, nodding blooms, and lapland diapensia, its tiny green cushions of leaves studded with big white blossoms. He stoked our small fire with the roots of heather, its stored resins sputtering and smoking.

There was also something reverent in the way Ipeelie stalked a seal, moving swiftly when it dozed, freezing when it looked up, concluding the hunt successfully in fifteen minutes. He gets a hundred seals a year, selling the skins for twenty dollars each; the meat goes to his fellow villagers and his dogs. (He himself can't eat seal meat, the Eskimo mainstay, but delights in boiled kelp as well as seafood cocktail from a walrus stomach.) He sells polar bear skins for two hundred dollars a foot, measured from nose to tail.

From the time Ipeelie was a baby, his parents coached him in the arts of survival. His father told him, for example, that really dangerous bears have black ears or appear to when the ears are flattened back. From his own observation, he knows about seals and their subniveous lairs: the haul-out lair for resting adults, the birth lair, and the nursing lair. He has watched bears so sated with young seals that they toss them into the air like footballs. He has studied bear tracks, and concludes that a seal is generally doomed when it allows a bear within fifty feet.

Ipeelie respects the polar bear's innua and the innua of all other life about him. As we spoke together, we watched the sun roll slowly around the horizon, moving a bit higher during midday and bringing a thousand ringed seals and a few bearded seals out onto the ice. Ipeelie tried again for a seal, but one after another slid into the water as we approached. His response was the same as it had been to other disappointments. He simply shrugged his shoulders, smiled and said, "Oh well." A man like that is untroubled by a temporary defeat.

Since he is educated and speaks English, shouldn't he represent Allen Island in establishing property claims? "If I do, then all I think of is that. I would not be happy."

He recently flew across the continent to British Columbia for a three-day seminar on arctic marine science. "Most boring time of my life," he said. "Sat all day and took notes. Terrible. Really terrible."

Ipeelie loves the ancient communal life. "When we get a walrus, we don't keep it to ourselves, we cut it up for everyone." What about lazy people? "There are no lazy people. We all hunt. We are all one big happy family,"—then he paused and smiled—"except my dogs and Uncle Lucashi's. They don't get along."

Such is the life of the Eskimo untouched by the modern world, or at least resistant to it. Only a few such villages remain in the arctic, as oil and mineral exploration is penetrating the remotest reaches.

In 1981, I visited all the Eskimo villages on the north and west coasts of Hudson Bay, traveling with my friend Keith Rawlings, who was trying to recruit workers for a gold mine at Cullaton Lake west of Eskimo Point. Only a few years back, these people had been nomads, living in skin tents in summer and snowhouses in winter. But during periods of famine, the Canadian government intervened with both shelter and emergency food, and what had been seasonal camps eventually became permanent villages, complete with a governing body of council members, chosen by ballot.

Hardly a village now is without television and dial phones, connected by satellite with other exchanges. Just imagine: from snowhouses to central heating, from blubber lamps to electric lights—in little more than a dozen years! The ability to cope with such a quantum leap into the modern world is a tribute to the Eskimo's intelligence. Those who went to work at a nearby nickel mine at Rankin Inlet proved to be quick, adaptable, and dependable. But when we tried to persuade them to work in the gold mines, very few were interested, even though the wages were tremendous and they would have to work only two weeks out of the month. Why should they leave home and hunting? They had their fiberglass boats, outboard motors, and snow machines—what else in life did they need?

The Eskimos of the Canadian arctic are still wonderfully friendly, magnificent people, as much a part of the northern sea ice as the polar bear. They have survived the most uncompromising environment in the northern hemisphere and have taken on the age of electronics with style and dignity, but they cannot withstand the battery of lawyers teaching hate—to people who have been singularly without it. Not long ago, the people of Barrow, Alaska, were among my favorites in the world: happy, outgoing, hospitable to strangers. But lawyers, posing as friends, have taught them a litany of grievances, eyeing settlement fees that run into millions of dollars. Two young white men were recently killed without apparent provocation at Duck Point, east of town. The bus driver warned me not to go there.

The harsh but idyllic world of Ipeelie Inookie and his friends, perhaps unparalleled in modern times, is probably already doomed.

A maternity den. In November the female digs in and soon gives birth, emerging in March. We searched for three years before we found this one south of Churchill.

For the first year, cubs must depend completely on their mother for food and protection.

Cubs stay as close as shadows to their mother.

There are frequent stops
to rest. Sometimes they
ride her back.

Few mothers are more af-
fectionate or loyal.

A mother picks up a dan-
gerous scent: an approaching bear. Generally she
flees, but this time her
nose tells her it is not a big
male.

The stranger is a juvenile. The mother lowers her head and freezes, a threatening stance, while her cubs watch anxiously.

Concerned for her cubs, she looks back and is reassured. Mothers with cubs are furious antagonists and sometimes fight to the death to save them.

The battle is won without a skirmish. She chases off the subadult. Now to resume hunting. Cubs, in their two years with her, have much to learn.

Spunky was an orphan at the Churchill dump. When she growled, bears ten times her 50-pound size retreated, unaware she had no mother to back up her bluff.

But with the onset of winter, there was no hope for her survival. When she was darted and tagged, all other bears had left for the ice.

Glassy-eyed, she was carried off, crated, and flown to the Winnipeg Zoo, where she made an instant hit. "That little cub is a treasure," we were told.

In Winnipeg Spunky captivated her keepers. "She loves everybody and is already right at home." But a call came from Ireland for polar bears.

Now in the Dublin Zoo, she has a playmate, Ootek, to romp and wrestle with. The orphan of the Churchill dump is now the darling of Dublin.

The Eskimo
Hunt

The Norwegian explorer Knud Rasmussen asked an elderly Eskimo what he considered the greatest happiness of his life. The man replied, "To run across fresh bear tracks and be ahead of all other sledges."

The old-time hunts by dog team and stone-tipped spear are over, but as long as there are fathers and grandfathers to tell about them, they will never be forgotten. They were perilous affairs, but as necessary for spirit as for body.

Eivind Astrup, in his book, *With Peary near the Pole*, told about a famous bear hunter, Akpallia, who was seized with the urge to revisit his old hunting ground in Melville Bay. There he teamed up with three local hunters, and, while his companions took the track of a female and cubs, he followed a single track. He saw the bear half a mile away. "Takkotakko! Takkotakko!" ("Look! Look!") he said to his five sled dogs, who couldn't see it. "Nanook, Nanook, Nanook, Kanooksuia!" ("A bear, a bear, a bear, a big bear!") The bear moved off and so did the dogs, in a frenzy.

Akpallia, a big man, jumped off the sledge to lighten it, holding tight to the handles. The bear was fast but, like all big bears encumbered by fat, no distance runner. Soon Akpallia jumped back on the sledge to save his strength.

As the dogs neared the bear, he slashed the traces and the pack flew on, holding the bear at bay as Akpallia ran forward, lance in hand. With both hands he thrust the spear at the bear, which turned and blunted the strike, then broke the spear in two and struck at the hunter. As Akpallia reached for his knife he sank through the snow crust. The bear was on him. Akpallia howled into the bear's open mouth to frighten it and struck with his fist, but he couldn't get loose. The dogs rushed to the attack. One quick stab of the bear's paw hurled off one dog, killing it instantly. Then from behind an ice cliff, another bear appeared, pursued by Akpallia's friends. When they shouted, the bear released him and ran away, and Akpallia survived.

In the bear hunt, Astrup concluded, "Life itself was the stake; food and clothing for a short period the coveted prize."

In the terse, graphic language of the Eskimo, Dan Leavitt told me what befell a friend of his father's. "They go to hunt seals and my father lose him. When he find him, all he see is his parky, turned inside out like a sock so the bear can eat every speck of him. Nothing else left. That bear ate that man all off."

Peter Freuchen has told of Eskimos who attacked bears with spears even when they had guns, and sometimes with no more than a knife. Was this bravado no more than a chance to show off to their friends? I found the stories hard to believe until I visited with Eskimos at every village along the west coast of Hudson Bay—Eskimo Point, Whale Cove, Rankin Inlet, Chesterfield Inlet and Baker Lake—and to the north, at Coral Harbour on Southampton Island and at Repulse Bay. The friendliness of the Eskimos was overwhelming; their stories were unembellished. There was hardly a man among them who hadn't killed a polar bear, some by spears and even knives because ammunition was often dangerously short and was consequently reserved for emergencies, to be used only to avert starvation.

As I flew north by chartered plane, I spoke with Andre Tautu of Chesterfield Inlet, an urbane-looking man of perhaps forty who is public relations chief of a small local airline. Out on a hunt with his father, Andre killed his first bear when he was nine. That night his grandmother threw a big party for all who could squeeze inside the igloo. "From that day," he said, "I was no longer a boy. I was finally a man."

For the hunt, Alaskan Eskimos sometimes used four-foot bows of spruce with braided sinews and two-foot spruce arrows armed with a flint blade fitted into a barbed arrowhead made of antlers. However, spearing was the traditional method. Their spears, five to six feet long, were often tipped with jade, whereas Eskimos across the Bering Strait in Siberia often used copper tips. The harpoon head for bears was much longer than that used for seals.

Ipeelie Inookie told me that his grandfather used a knife for hunting bears, even when he had a gun. "He wrestled with bears, just for the fun of it," he said, shaking his head. "I wouldn't wrestle a bear for anything." Ipeelie has seen the arms and chest of a man who wrestled with a polar bear. "All scars," he said. "Really terrible."

Van de Velde describes more recent hunts. He says bears that have never before encountered a hunter, or those suffering from extreme hunger won't hesitate to attack a man, and Eskimos generally allow such bears to come up very close. "When he charges," the priest says, "he gallops sideways like a dog. The hunter awaits the proper moment and then flashes the harpoon into the animal's neck, quickly shifting to one side as the bear passes. If the aim is accurate enough, it will reach the spinal nerve."[21]

Leo Kaludjak of Whale Cove told me how at nineteen he speared a bear with an eight-foot lance, an event so routine that he hardly remembers the details. The bear charged, galloping up and tipping its head on one side; as he jumped to the opposite side, he speared it back of the shoulder.[22]

In *We Don't Live in Snow Houses Now*, printed by an Eskimo cooperative, Andrew Oyukuluk of Arctic Bay tells how, in his youth, he killed one bear with a spear and another with a knife. "We had no guns then," he said, "and I had no idea how strong they were. One time while the dogs worried a bear, I crept up on him and slipped a cord around his neck. He was so strong he bounced me off at first, but I finally choked him while he was attacking me with his claws." He continues sadly, "Now I am very slow and deathly afraid of them."

Granny Rosa Konayok of Repulse Bay, barely five feet tall and weighing no more than ninety pounds, believes she was born near Pelly Bay but doesn't know how old she is.[23] Rosa bore no children, so often when her husband was away, she went out seal hunting on her own. A successful hunt was a joyous occasion to her, because like most older Eskimos she has often been near starvation. She outlived her three husbands. She was out hunting with her second husband, who was nearly blind, when she shot her first polar bear. She shot a second when it threatened to come inside her tent. Rosa adopted five children and now lives with her grandson and his family in a government-owned house at Repulse Bay. A granddaughter, who has also spent most of her life in igloos and skin tents, translated for us as the wind outside howled and the thermometer showed 35° below zero. As we spoke, little Granny smoked one cigarette after another.

She was out with her brother one day when a bear charged them. They had two dogs with them, a male and female; only the male stood up to the bear. Her brother's only weapon was a knife with a six-inch blade. The bear moved swiftly towards them, and as he came up close, he tipped his head on one side and opened his mouth wide. Her brother quickly jumped to the other side and plunged the knife several times between the bear's ribs, killing it. Was her brother hurt? Granny paused to think. She couldn't remember. Then she brightened. "But I do remember that he said he had trouble getting out of bed the next morning."

Everywhere across the arctic I had asked Eskimos why a bear charges with his head averted in the manner she described. Granny told me the probable reason. "The bear see that tall, straight-up animal and thinks he must tip his head to bite across it."

She also explained that the speed of a charging bear is such that he cannot swerve fast enough to grab the hunter who moves aside. Had there been a team of dogs, Granny said, they would have engaged the bear and allowed her brother a margin of safety.

As we spoke, Granny would look out the window of her warm, comfortable home. She longed for the old days, she said, for traveling by dog team and sled to distant villages to see her friends and relatives, but even more she longed for the chance to walk across the tundra in summertime, rifle in hand, looking for caribou.

One of the most famous hunters of Coral Harbour is Mikitok Bruce, a handsome Eskimo of fifty-seven, who, like Granny, has spent most of his life in skin tents in summer and snowhouses in winter heated by a pair of *qudliqs* (soapstone lamps), one on each side of the bed. While several of his grandchildren clambered across his lap, Bruce spoke of his hunting, while his beautiful daughter translated. He was tired, having just come back from killing a walrus the night before, but he was happy to talk.

My father didn't teach me well. On my first hunt we saw thirty seals near a breathing hole. He said to run in and put a piece of polar bear skin over the hole to block it off, but the seals dived at me and I harpooned only one. All the time I lived with my father he told me I would never be a good hunter.

It was my grandfather who taught me hunting. You must approach a seal cautiously by crawling up, all the time making different kinds of sounds, spanking the ice or rubbing the snow, making sounds like seals, geese, eiders, loons, and the like. If you make the same sound, they get suspicious. He showed me how to lie on a piece of polar bear skin, fur-side down. Wrapped in it, you crawl sideways towards the seal. Often a single pull of the arm lets you slide forward ten feet. Hunting like this is quiet and you don't get wet. Since I started hunting this way, I have sometimes killed thirty seals at one ice crack.

On my first polar bear hunt with my father, we saw two bears on the hill just above the seashore. Slowly I crawled up until I thought I was close enough and aimed and fired, but missed. I missed a second shot, too, but hit with my third shot. My father came up, angry at me for not getting closer and for wasting ammunition. He said that a wounded bear often escapes by swimming across open water.

My father would sometimes come up within five feet before he fired. One day he saw a big male and decided to crawl up on it. When he was only three or four feet away, he shot it in the hip, a good place to fire because only its head flung up. If you shoot it in the chest it may rear up and attack you and this can be dangerous.

If you see a bear den during winter, you need not worry—just be careful. As you approach it, be sure your dogs haven't scattered snow over the hole. To find out if the bear is inside, poke your mitt or rifle case into the hole. This will draw him out. If you wound a bear in the den you must enter and kill it, and this is risky. Once I saw my dogs go over to a den and stop. Suddenly a bear came out. The dogs hadn't even noticed it. It began to chase me and I realized my rifle was under the tarp on my komatik. But as fast as it appeared, it returned to its den. The dogs dug away. I aimed at the bear's legs and fired as it came out. It could have bitten me if it had wanted to, but instead it lunged at the dogs.

A group of dogs confound a bear and he sits on his haunches to protect his rear. He is normally so occupied that a hunter can move in fast for a shot or a spear thrust. But bears learn fast and soon find they can run away and up to the top of an ice cliff, where they can look down on dogs. You must get it quick or it will get away.

Mikitok has killed three bears with a spear. When I asked him what kind he had used, he went outside to the porch and brought in the blood-smeared spear he had used on the walrus the day before. It was a wooden pole about four and a half feet long with a foot-long iron prong.

Without dogs, the danger in spearing a bear is infinitely greater. Mikitok's grandfather was caught without dogs when a bear charged him. He crouched and planted the end of his eight-foot spear firmly in the snow, the sharp end aimed directly at the bear, who ran right into the point.

Van de Velde tells of Nilaulak and his wife, two of his parishioners, who were riding along shore on their sled in early December when they saw a bear. After the dogs were cut loose, they cornered the bear on a patch of newly formed ice. Nilaulak ran to the animal and speared it, but as the bear shifted its weight to bite at the spear, the ice crumbled, dropping bear, dogs, and man into the water. The bear grabbed Nilaulak but could not bite through his parka of double-lined caribou skins. Eventually the man worked his way free and, with the help of his wife, pulled himself onto solid ice. Hurriedly he hitched up his dogs and raced for home, a few miles away, his clothing a shell of ice around his body. It took him three days to dry his clothes over the small flame of an oil lamp. Later he found the bear carcass. He set traps and caught several foxes.

Simon Inuksak, in an article in the September 1957 issue of *Eskimo* magazine (published by the Oblate Fathers of the Hudson Bay Vicarate), tells of encountering bears in their dens. He was making a trip to Amittok when his dogs caught scent of a bear.

> I cut them loose and taking my harpoon shaft I probed the bear's igloo. The bear bit at it. I cut an opening and struck the bear a blow. But lo and behold! He came out. I hit him again then ran back to get my harpoon head and fix it to the shaft. Now when I threw the harpoon at him, he fell. I finished him off with my knife. Another time I found an open igloo. I harpooned the bear through the door but didn't kill him. I ran because the bear had the harpoon between his teeth and I had no more weapons. I returned the next day and brought down the bear. There it is. That's all.

Hunting was hazardous, especially during the dark winter days when the sun never rose and snow came in blinding sheets. Dogs would race headlong after a bear, the komatik slamming behind. In the dark, all a hunter could do was hold on and hope the sled got stuck in the ice. If he had the chance, he cut loose his best dogs and waited for the bark that meant the bear was at bay. Sometimes a bear turned on the hunter.

Bellarmine Lafortune, a priest on King Island, wrote in his diary about one of his parishioners who had wounded a bear.

> This time the animal did a thing that very few of them do, turning volte-face and coming right back on his aggressor. Frank knew he had three cartridges in his gun. He first stood his ground and shot the infuriated beast but did not disable it. He shot a second time without more effect. Probably due to excitement, he missed his third shot. The bear was within a few feet of him. He had no time to reload. Then began a race in comparison with which all marathon races are child's play. If fear ever gave wings, it was this time. The frightful gnarling of the wounded beast became more and more distinct. The crunching of its claws and its breath could be heard easily. One or two minutes more and a slap of its left paw would have hurled Frank into eternity. But lo! Comes Kunnuk, a companion, running like a wild deer. In a wink he threw his knapsack on the ice, grabbed a gun, aimed, and blazed. The inert mass of the victim rolled within two feet of Frank. May the Sacred Heart be blessed forever!

Guns made life easier, but there were still dangers. Often a hunter sleeping in his camp would be awakened in the middle of the night by a bear prowling about the room. "Many hunters I know," says Van de Velde, "without taking time to dress just leaped for their guns—always left outside to avoid frost—and standing naked and barefooted in the snow downed the visitor."

The charm of an Eskimo story is that seldom does the narrator make himself a hero; sometimes he is even the butt of a joke. Nuligak had been out after seals when he suddenly saw three bears. He promptly unhitched three of his dogs. As he approached one of the bears, it charged, and he fired several shots, but missed. "A bear coming straight at you is a poor target," he explains. "I had five cartridges left. I put one in the gun. The bear was seven feet from me when I shot and killed her outright." But that night in the igloo, he began to feel strange. The footsteps of his children startled him and he hid behind his wife. "Fear had caught up with me," he said. "Everyone burst out laughing."

Stories like these, besides being entertainment, were education in the arts of survival. "We Inuit learn from our parents what they tell us," one Eskimo said to *Alaska* magazine. "The memories of our old men are our encyclopedia."

An Eskimo boy became a man on the day he killed his first polar bear, and the same is still true today. On a flight to Eskimo Point, a young man, Peter Pangonauk, told me that he was sitting in his ninth grade classroom when he looked out of the window and saw a bear. He jumped up and ran home for his gun and shot it. There was celebrating in his house that night—a giant feast for everyone who could get inside.

Muckpaloo (he has no other name that anyone knows), born in 1939 in a camp called Sinnasiuvik outside Arctic Bay, started going along on hunting expeditions at age six, caring for the dogs. Shortly after, when his stepfather died, he went out trapping, fishing, and seal hunting by himself. His mother told him he should never sit around when he could be hunting. When he killed his first seal, he couldn't pull it up through the ice and had to get his brother's help. He shot his first polar bear when he was nine.

Eskimo women liked to hunt bears and did so when they weren't occupied with children—which was rare. More often they were forced to shoot bears in self-defense. In the spring of 1956, Lucie Imingmak, a member of Father Van de Velde's parish, was at home with her two-year-old son while her husband and older son were seal hunting. Lucie, a semi-invalid from polio, was expecting a baby. She crawled outside, thinking she heard her husband's sled, and saw a bear running towards the tent. Lucie grabbed the old gun by the opening of the tent and waited. She recognized a young male, starved and thin. When he was within a hundred feet, she took up the musket, aimed, and fired. Wounded to death, the bear fell. Lucie looked into the tent and found the baby still asleep.

Bears sometimes enter the porch, where provisions are kept, breaking down a wall or a window. Van de Velde says, "I have known many women home alone who, instead of losing their wits, tossed the bear bits of grease and food until the bear would walk away or lie down near the igloo to digest his free meal."

An Eskimo told my brother, who lived for a time at Barrow, Alaska, the following story, which, though it sounds like legend, he vouched was true:

> One day I spear a seal but too tired to drag him home. I tell my wife to go get him. She go with her little dog and find a bear eating the seal. She spear him and another

bear come up and she spear him too. She come back home and say, "I too tired. Go get my bear and your seal." I no believe her. Finally I go out and see her two bears! What a woman!

Ipeelie, in the same spare language, told us:

My ma shot a bear in our camp. She tried to scare him away but he wouldn't go. So she finished his life. No choice but to kill it. When we men were away at Frobisher working in the fall of 1976, nine bears came into camp and stayed all week. As soon as we came back, no more bears.

For as far back as anyone can remember, tradition dictated that whoever first saw a bear—man, woman, or child—got to keep the skin. Even before the day of inflated prices, the skin of a polar bear was a real prize. A big one would make three pairs of men's trousers, and polar bear pants worn fur-side out were prestigious garments. The long hair of the forelegs was carefully saved to trim the tops of women's boots. The longer the hair, the better; a wife advertised her husband's hunting prowess with her boots. In the days when Peter Freuchen lived among the Eskimos, the skin might be sold intact, but the decision to do so was a hard one, said Freuchen, "for it implies that a hunter is so poor at trapping foxes that he must cheat his friends of their trousers."

Rasmussen, too, noted the Eskimo's esteem for his polar bear trousers and his contempt for men who couldn't keep themselves in proper pants. Bear skin was scarce but indispensable. In *Across Arctic America*, he writes:

Without warm bear skin trousers it would be impossible to undertake long journeys in winter time; and where there is no bear-hunting there will be no proper bunk rugs to lie on. The hunters on the windward side therefore characterize the lee-side inhabitants, with some malice, as kitchen hunters who in spite of their wealth of meat and their fat dogs, have to trade for bear skin with the real hunters.

The Polar Eskimos who comprise the world's most northerly settlement (near Thule Air Base) still wear pants made of polar bear skin, and at prevailing prices such pants are worth a thousand dollars apiece. Fred Bruemmer, the writer-photographer, lived with the Polar Eskimos for two months, and since he couldn't afford to buy a pair of such pants, he rented a pair for two hundred dollars, to check on their effectiveness as a winter garment. They provided excellent insulation when he sat for most of a day over icy waters in the bottom of a kayak. But after they got wet, the pants grew stiff and chafed his skin, something that didn't appear to bother his Eskimo friends.

Bear skins were also indispensible to the Eskimo's beds, providing both insulation and softness. Even small pieces of skin were valued in times past, particularly for icing the runners of komatiks, which were first covered with moist earth—generally peat—which was allowed to freeze, then planed smooth. Then the Eskimo sprayed the bear skin with a mouthful of water and either rubbed the runners with it or shook the water from it onto the runners. The oily fur held the water just long enough; nothing else seemed to work as well.

To muffle the sound of their steps on a seal hunt, Eskimos made big overshoes of bear hide, fur side down, to slip over their boots. They made shields that looked like umbrellas from polar bear and these they pushed ahead of them when they stalked a seal. Some of these shields they mounted on runners equipped with bear skins.

After a successful bear hunt, the meat was generally apportioned throughout the camp. Eskimos of Hudson Bay with whom I spoke are fond of it. Mary Amougauk of Whale Cove says, "It's my most famous [favorite] meat." People on Banks Island, who have a plentiful supply of caribou and musk-oxen, prefer those animals. At Churchill, bear meat is scorned by Chipewyans, who call it dog food only, and this disdain is perhaps what causes my friend Joe Kowal of the Polar Inn to say of it, "My taste buds say yes but my stomach says no."

Freuchen spoke of sharing a pot of bear meat with his Eskimo friends, each one drinking deeply of the soup, which he said "tastes strong and spicy as it goes down. When nobody wanted more soup, the owner of the pot always had a dog that needed something extra for the road."

Until a generation or two ago, explorers ate raw bear meat, not realizing the grave danger of trichinosis. Freuchen said it was like eating raw oysters. To Stefansson, chewing half-frozen bear meat was like eating hard ice cream.[24]

It is strange that more Eskimos did not suffer or die from trichinosis, since only in relatively recent times has the incidence of trichina in polar bears been publicized. Trichinosis is a frightful disease. A longtime priest of the arctic, Father Hubert Mascaret, now at Coral Harbour, told me about his experiences with it.[25] He was at Ivugivit, a tiny village on the northern tip of Quebec, when eight Eskimos came down with trichinosis after eating raw bear meat. He telegraphed Ottawa, asking what he should do.

> I shall never forget the answer a doctor wired back: "Nothing can be done." It was that day that my hair started turning white. But I cared for them, and slowly they got better, though sometimes they were out of their heads. Apparently they had not taken in enough trichina to kill them.

Polar bear liver, because of its high content of Vitamin A, is now generally believed to be poisonous. In several experiments by Stefansson and a few of his party, some took sick with headaches and nausea, while others didn't. Stefansson wondered whether Eskimos warned him against the liver not because it was poisonous, but because it was taboo and eating it would bring misfortune. Sometimes the man would die from eating it, Eskimos told him; more often, within a year one of his relatives would contract leucodermia, a whitening of the skin fairly common among Eskimos, as well as Africans. Stefansson found an old man with three-fourths of his skin white; other Eskimos said he had eaten bear liver as a child, something he denied. Dogs that chance to eat polar bear liver lose all their hair, according to my Eskimo friends; the liver of lake fish has the same effect.

Hunting was in full swing at Repulse Bay when I stopped there in March 1981.

Bears were moving over the ice, especially at Wager Bay a hundred miles south, where several men had gone by snow machine to hunt. One hunter whose machine broke down had been forced to stay out all night in a raging storm at 35° below zero, and when search parties found him the next morning before daylight he was walking toward town; nobody even asked how he had spent the night, it was all so common. At Coral Harbour, the hunt had ended, with a full quota of sixty-five bears, the biggest quota by far of all in Canada, and fifty-five of the skins were at the Hudson's Bay store, awaiting shipment to the fur auction. There was an air of excitement.

Before the advent of hunting by snow machine, the old-time hunt was more than excitement; killing a bear was for the hunter more than something to boast about; it was an experience somehow ennobling, a union with the spirit forces in the world about him. I have asked my friend Wayne Born to tell about the hunt. Wayne is a missionary, educator, and pilot, who lived among the Eskimos for eighteen years and often flew food in to starving villages. He is a big red-haired, soft-spoken man, who is anything but bloodthirsty. He and his wife have reared several Eskimo children along with their own three, and have legally adopted two Eskimos, a son, and a daughter who was given them when she was only three hours old.

When word came that traditional Eskimo hunting would be outlawed the following year, Wayne realized that if his oldest son, Ray, were to experience the heritage of the hunt as his ancestors knew it, it must be now. They set out with Timothy Lennie, a famous bear-hunter of Holman Island, on a last great bear-hunt, to a place on the north side of Victoria Island where few hunters dared come because, long before anyone could ever remember, a lost tribe of "little people" had built houses out of slabs of rock that still stand, unmarred by centuries of cold.

Wayne tells the story of the hunt.

We set out, each of us with a team of eight dogs and sleds and for the next three weeks we left other humans far behind as we traveled to Glenelg Bay. Our big, wonderful dogs were as eager as we were for the trail. We followed the coast and from time to time would climb some high point and check the surrounding ice with fieldglasses. When we saw a bear we would watch to see what he was doing, then decide very quietly what we were going to do. Very carefully and deliberately, so as not to excite the dogs, we would take our camping gear off the sleds and stow it, then cut loose our two trained bear dogs and start off. When the teams felt the lightened sled behind them they would take off at a furious pace, their heads all up and their tails like flags, racing over smooth ice and rough, so we could barely hang on. All of a sudden the dogs would smell or else see the bear and the two loose dogs would start after it. Generally the bear would run, perhaps mistaking the dogs for a pack of wolves. Young bears would keep on running, often so fast they'd leave us behind. Older bears, knowing they couldn't get away, would try to climb some cliff of ice or rock. We'd grab our ice anchors and slam them into the hard snow to try stopping the team so we could get a shot before the free dogs caught up with him.

There is nothing like it in the world. I know of nothing more dangerous or exciting. We were three hundred miles from the nearest humans, in an area we'd never before seen, in a place where people hadn't lived for fifty years, and where anything might happen—and did. The cache of food that Lennie had put up in the fall was gone when we got to it; bears had eaten up everything. That's when we prayed. And that afternoon we saw our first bears and got three. For five days we lived on boiled bear meat. In the north there is always the chance that you might lose your dogs or that in the chase your sleds break up. You must cross deep crevasses. Our only safety lay in having three teams, so if something happened to some of the dogs or sleds, we'd have others. Sometimes when we worked our way up over tremendous piles of ice we came face to face with a bear.

The bears undoubtedly had never before seen a man.[26] One old bear defied us. He refused to run. He was big and fat and strong; there were plenty of seals around. He had many patches of black skin showing. He let us come right up to him.

A bear's power and speed going up the face of what seems like a perpendicular cliff is incredible. He's suddenly on top and looking down on you. You don't go after a bear above you. He can move too fast for you to take a chance.

During their last long hunt, they killed seven bears and Timothy trapped thirty white foxes. They traveled some nine hundred miles.

To Wayne Born, a gentle man, there is nothing wrong with such a hunt.

Indeed, there is something noble—even spiritual—about the true hunt. My greatest moments in the north have come as I watched a hunter with his dogs and komatik far, far off, coming toward home. All the villagers too would be watching, some from their rooftops. We would try to make out if the hunter's komatik was well loaded or empty. We knew what starvation meant. As the hunter moved closer we would see that he was heavily loaded. We were jubilant. People would jump down from the roofs and we would all shout with joy. After the hunter had emptied his komatik and put his dogs away, his wife would come out and invite in the whole village. "Neregata neregiti!" she would call. "Because we eat, all of us eat!"[27]

There is the same kind of reverence in Nuligak's account of how a bear fed his starving family.

My children got very little to eat at times. February 9th was one of those times. No open water. I left anyhow and far out I saw a polar bear. I killed it; I was so happy thinking that the children would have something to eat that I never forgot that day I killed a male white bear, big and fat. I cut it up, chose a piece of meat from the paws, and put it in my bag. I gave it to Stanley, my youngest, when he came to meet me. "Go and show this to your mother." This he did, and Margaret shouted with joy. . . . With my forty-four cartridges, from January to March, I killed thirty seals, five *ugiuk*, the big bearded seals, and four white bears. I am not saying this to brag nor to serve as an example to younger men, but only to stress that I was very happy to have changed my cartridges into so many things to eat.

To Nuligak and other traditional Eskimos the hunt was a noble tragedy of awe and fear mixed with joy.

I often think of my white bear hunts, and the joy I had when I found fresh tracks. I can still see the dogs running freely on the trail. We follow them and there, not too far ahead, they begin to bark. We are happy then! They get after the bear, circle about it and bite its haunches. It becomes impossible for the bear to escape. Can anyone forget moments like these?

Other animals gave the Eskimo more actual return than the bear. Seals, walrus, and whales gave him blubber for food, light, and heat, skins for clothing and tents, sinews for sewing, entrails for making waterproof garments and bags, and bones and tusks for making weapons, cooking utensils, and art objects. But it was the polar bear that conferred prestige, a symbol of the hunter's bravery and prowess. Killing a bear was the ultimate achievement of a man's life, and the scars he sometimes incurred were a lasting badge of his courage.

But all this is changing. Ipeelie says, "Now that we have guns and skidoos, polar bears aren't dangerous at all. The thrill of the hunt is over." According to Father Mascaret: "To Eskimos, the polar bear is no longer a big, noble animal, a creature of folklore. They see dollar bills on him." Peter and Elisapee Kanangnaq Ahlooloo of Arctic Bay say that their whole world is changing.

> Once Inuit used to help each other. If someone had no food, the rest would send meat. If somebody got a seal, everybody would come and the meat would be divided. When we would gather at a dance, we would find out who had food and who didn't. Today it is not like that. Some people have plenty of caribou and other meat and some have absolutely nothing. Oingunn, one of the best hunters, brings meat to the older people, but many adults think only of themselves, and share only with their immediate families.

Mikitok Bruce shook his head sadly as he spoke. "People seem to have changed so much. They live too freely. They don't care about the future. They are just breathing."

06

How Dangerous Are They?

Perhaps the best answer to the question of how dangerous a polar bear is comes from the author Ernest Thompson Seton.

> Before me is a pile of data dealing with the moods and temper of the [polar] bear. One portion proves that the creature is timid, flying always from man, shunning an encounter with him at any price. The other maintains that the white bear fears nothing in the north, knowing that he is king; and is just as ready to enter a camp of Eskimos or a ship of white men as to attack a crippled seal.

Even the old explorers couldn't agree on how dangerous polar bears were. Norwegian and Finnish harpooners called spearing bears a noble and dangerous sport, but an old Danish guide called killing a bear no more dangerous than killing a sheep.

Early explorers expected almost any polar bear that saw or scented them to walk up without hesitation for a closer look. A Norwegian explorer, A. E. Nordenskiøld, who traveled around Asia and Europe in his ship in the late 1860s, described in *The Voyage of the Vega* how bears would nose around tents on shore and swim out to his boat as it lay at anchor. And though striking a match was enough to scare off one bear, most of them would stalk the crew.

> When he observes a man he commonly approaches in hope of prey, with supple movements, and in a hundred zigzag bends, in order to conceal the direction he intends to take, and thus keep his prey from being frightened. During his approach he often climbs up on blocks of ice, or raises himself on his hind legs, in order to get a more extensive view, or else stands snuffing up the air with evident care in all directions. . . . If he thinks he has to do with a seal, he creeps or trails himself forward along the ice. . . . If one keeps quite still, the bear comes in this way so near that one can shoot him at the distance of two gun-lengths, or, what the hunters consider safer, kill him with the lance. If an unarmed man falls in with a polar bear, some rapid movements and loud cries are generally sufficient to put him to flight, but if the man himself flees, he is certain to have the bear after him at full speed. If the bear is wounded, he always takes to flight. He often lays snow upon the wound with his fore-paws.

Another early traveler, returning to his tent from a Hudson Bay post in 1789, passed through a thicket of willows, awakening a bear. With nothing to defend himself, he held his pack sack in front of him. The bear smelled the bag, which held a loaf of bread and a rundlet of beer, and walked quietly away, "thereby relieving the man from his very disagreeable situation."

Stefansson concluded that, "with all their strength and splendid weapons of teeth and claws, they are generally retiring." But as with so many generalizations about polar bears, the exceptions all but equal the rule.

Two Eskimos near Point Hope were tending their seal nets during the winter of 1880, according to an account by Edward W. Nelson, whose ethnographic notes form a remarkable collection at the Smithsonian.

> One of the men heard a bear approaching over the frosty snow, and having no weapon but a small knife, the bear being between him and the shore, he threw himself upon his back on the ice and waited. The bear came up in a few moments, and smelled about the man from head to foot, and finally pressed his cold nose against the man's lips and nose, and sniffed several times; each time, the terrified Eskimo held his breath until, as he afterwards said, his lungs nearly burst. The bear suddenly heard the other man at work, and listening for a moment, he started towards him at a gallop, while the man he left sprang to his feet, and ran for his life for the village, and reached it safely. At midday when the sun had risen a little above the horizon, a large party went out to the spot, and found the bear finishing his feast upon the other hunter. Cases similar to this occur occasionally all along the coast where the bear is found in winter.
>
> A number of Eskimo on the Alaskan coast show frightful scars obtained in contests with them in winter. One man, who came on board the *Corwin*, had the entire skin and flesh torn from one side of his head and face, including the eye and ear, yet had escaped and recovered.

With food around, bears are anything but retiring. Not long ago, the crew of a Canadian Coast Guard ship amused themselves by tossing a bear a carton of molasses, jam, salt pork, salami, chocolate bars, and a jar of peanut butter, which he licked out in a few mouthfuls. Then he stuck his head in a porthole, asking for more. At a sister ship, after being thrown a steak, the bear climbed aboard, to the dismay of the crew, since he was a big male marked with fighting scars. When the crew turned hoses on him, he loved it and raised his paws to get the stream under his armpits! Only a rocket fired next to him moved him off.

How do polar bears compare in temperament with their closest relatives, the grizzlies? Almost everyone who knows them both will testify that polar bears are for the most part more amiable than grizzlies, who are generally irritable and ready to charge, living up to their Latin name, *Ursus horribilis*.[28] Grizzlies fight when any of three things are threatened: themselves, their food supply, or their cubs. Unlike polar bears, they are strongly territorial and contend to keep out intruders; a grizzly's first impulse when it sees a strange bear—or man—is to make a charge.

Stirling believes that polar bears are much more tractable than grizzlies. They don't easily get upset, and around people, they don't react so quickly. Lentfer agrees; in tagging eight hundred bears, only once did he have to defend himself, when the tranquilizing dart did not function properly and the bear charged within three feet of him and had to be shot. Lentfer notes that in recent years there have been no deaths in Alaska from polar bears, but several from blacks and grizzlies.

Another bear specialist qualified to compare polar bears and grizzlies is John J. Craighead, a longtime student of grizzlies, who led the Committee for Exploration and Research on a 1970 trip to North Twin Island in James Bay in 1970. In a brochure he writes that he and two companions watched a big male polar bear on North Twin Island standing in the shallow water offshore, head submerged and moving slowly back and forth as he searched for kelp, then surfacing with the seaweed in his paws. He ate daintily, turning each paw over to get the shreds from between his claws. Sometimes he submerged completely, blowing out bubbles as he went down, remaining below for up to a minute. Arctic terns dived at the bear constantly, and as he ate, he would pause and look up at them. After an hour, he came ashore and began moving towards the scientists, perhaps to return to his day bed on a grassy knoll behind them.

> He was only 75 feet away and we were between him and his bed. He could not scent us but raised his head several times. Twice he lowered his head and took a step forward. Each time the clicking of our cameras stopped him. I estimated him at 1,000 to 1,100 pounds. I talked softly to Derek and Johnny, hoping my voice would deter him. He definitely wanted to get past us to the point but was undecided. Once I was sure he was going to move on us and told Derek to hold the gun on his neck. I had the .375 pistol but didn't take it out of the holster. Twice he raised his head and hissed loudly. I moved a little and we all talked, saying "Go back, old boy." Very slowly he retreated backward step by step, always facing us. When about 75 feet out in the water he turned and swam off. It was an exciting encounter.

Another bear they came upon rose on his haunches and stared at them directly for thirty to forty seconds, then dropped limply to the ground and laid his head on his forepaws. Every few minutes he would raise his head, sniff the air and then lower his head to his paws. "He reminded me," says Craighead, "of a large lazy hound sacked out beside a fire—too comfortable to move."

Craighead concludes that the polar bear is normally a docile animal, bolder than a wild-living black bear and not nearly as aggressive or nervous as the grizzly.

> I would have been extremely apprehensive approaching a grizzly sow and cubs in the open to within 100 yards. I had no such apprehension approaching the polar bear. We carried no gun and the .375 sidearm was at the bottom of my pack. It is difficult to explain why I felt secure—somehow the behavior of the polar bear does not suggest aggressiveness, whereas the behavior of a grizzly does, and this behavior rings a bell in one's primitive instinct.

Obviously, denning females are dangerous. Lentfer was investigating a den, probing into it with a ski pole. He got no response, and started to crawl inside the long tunnel. When he was four feet in, he heard or felt—he doesn't know which—a big blast of air, then heard a growling sound. He back-pedaled out fast! Biologists generally give occupied maternity dens a wide berth.

Mothers with cubs are completely unpredictable. Brian Knudsen, a Canadian biologist studying bear behavior on North Twin Island in James Bay in the summer of 1970, was sitting with a friend in a cook-shack having a drink before supper. Knudsen told me what happened.

> My friend was sitting beside the open door—which opened out—when I heard him mutter something about bears. What I didn't know was that a bear had poked her head in within six inches of his left elbow and then slowly retired. I thought that he was telling me that he saw a bear down by the beach, so I got up, drink in hand, and went to the door.
>
> There, not ten feet off, was a mother and three cubs. The instant she saw me she charged, roaring and rearing up to full height, slamming against the door jamb so that the cabin shook. For a split second we stood eyeball to eyeball. All I could think of doing was to throw my drink and the plastic glass at her. That did it. She turned and ran off. My friend had found and lit a thunder-flash that I grabbed from his hand and threw. It landed just over the doorsill and exploded almost in my face, turning me coal black. By now the bears were down at the beach. I don't know why the bear didn't come inside except that the doorway was narrow and she may have thought it wasn't wide enough.

The summer before, Knudsen had been lying behind a ridge watching a snowy owl through his field glasses. A bear was sleeping, hidden in a small depression no more than ten feet away. It roused and stood.

> It came barreling out as I jumped to my feet. I waved my arms and shouted and began running backwards. The bear followed, hissing, which is a threat warning for bears. I kept shouting as I ran backwards. The bear could have got me with a single leap but didn't; instead he came running slowly, always about five feet away, his lips open. We ran this way for fifty yards before he finally turned and left me. He was a four to five hundred pound bear. I don't know why he didn't take me. Maybe I looked too big. Perhaps he saw me as a competitor rather than food. If either of those bears had been a grizzly, I feel sure I would have been mauled.

There was a polar bear on North Twin in the winter of 1971–72 that did stalk Knudsen almost constantly, an old female past thirty, as lean as a scarecrow, her teeth mostly gone and so arthritic she couldn't run.

> She didn't have a prayer of catching a seal. She wasn't afraid of rifle shots. She would look in our window and try the door of the cabin. We'd see her downwind of us, face to the wind. It was obvious she was hunting us. There wasn't a chance of her feeding herself and some day she might surprise us, so we disposed of her.

Knudsen says that the real danger from polar bears comes when they are startled. "Say you have a friendly thousand-pound basset hound and surprised him, you could get hurt, too. The same way. I'd hate to startle a big football player who was asleep."

The barking of dogs seems to ruffle a bear's usually placid temper. At Eskimo Point, a bear moved down a line of chained dogs, killing every one.[29] Foxes irritate him, too, and often before he settles down to eat, he will make repeated charges at foxes that are at least fifty yards away.

John Spence is a shy young Chipewyan whose left arm is off at the shoulder from an encounter with a polar bear. In March 1969 he had gone with his father and others on a beaver-trapping expedition to Owl Creek, south of Churchill, where shallow streams thread the taiga and willows crowd the banks. He was standing head down, checking a trap under a clump of willows, when out of nowhere a sledgehammer paw whammed his left side and raked his body as he fainted. When he came to, blood was spurting from his arm, and the bear was gone. Relatives raced him by dog team over the snow to McClintock, a stop on the Churchill railroad. A couple of days later, an Otter put down and flew him to Churchill, where a military plane relayed him to a hospital in Winnipeg. It is hard for him to tell exactly what happened, remembering the terror of his last days of trapping.

It is possible that a bear that attacks without provocation may be suffering from trichinosis. In humans, at least, a principal symptom is extreme muscle pain, and the worse the infection, the worse the pain. (Hogs on the other hand, show no symptoms.) When researchers checked a three-and-a-half-year-old grizzly that had killed a young woman in Glacier Park without apparent provocation, they found the highest trichina infection they had ever measured: 578 larvae to a single gram of flesh, or about ten times as high as the average of infected bears in the area. The relationship of aggression to infection is strictly a postulate. A nineteen-year-old grizzly that had killed a human a few years earlier had no more than a single trichina to a gram.

The fact remains that, despite the generally amiable disposition of the polar bear, he is profoundly dangerous, particularly when hungry.

In the dark of an arctic winter, two young men busied themselves aboard an oil-drilling barge frozen fast in the ice north of the Mackenzie River offshore in the Canadian Beaufort sea. The two decided to return to the mess hall for coffee. One didn't make it, and when his companion missed him he started a search, enlisting most of the seventy men on the vessel. They found scratch marks on the door of the sewage disposal plant where the missing youth worked.

At noon, as the darkness lifted slightly, the searchers found the missing man's head on the ice not far from the barge. Then they saw an eight-foot polar bear clutching the body. Nowhere in camp was there a gun. Regulations permit one firearm to a drill site camp, but some supervisors refuse to keep a weapon. "We tried firing a flare gun," said a fellow worker, "but it froze up. The bear would stand up and shake the body like a dog with a woodchuck. We chased him with a forklift but he moved off into the jagged ice where we couldn't follow. It was terrible to watch a man being eaten."

A gun flown in from another camp misfired. Only after a rifle from the Royal

In order to coexist, powerful predators develop an etiquette that is precise. Bears circle, evaluating one another's size and, probably, intentions.

The smaller bear sniffs ingratiatingly, but at first gets no response.

The big bear rises. There is no sound. Communication is purely by body language.

Wagging his head quickly from side to side, the big bear invites the other to play.

The invitation is declined, as is usual with bears of differing sizes.

The meeting is over. Each bear knows his relative rank in bear society.

After an hour of mock fighting, these siblings cooled off, then resumed play in the water. Sometimes both were submerged.

Ashore until hunting resumes, bears—even adult males—form lasting friendships, even to the point of sharing food.

When a stranger appears, the tranquility ends. Bear interactions are as stylized as a ballet.

They circle slowly, trying to get downwind. Bears probably recognize others by smell as well as sight.

There appears to be no room in the club for the stranger.

Two companions get ready to play. Adult females are rarely part of such a group.

Canadian Mounted Police was flown in was the bear killed. It turned out to be a two-year-old with a metal tag affixed to its ear.

A grisly story. Yet death by polar bear remains an extremely rare event, considering the stepped-up oil, gas, and mineral exploration throughout the arctic. In recent years, only three workers have been killed at drill sites, all by bears that appeared to be near starvation.

Across the Atlantic on 21 July 1977, at Svalbard, a party of Austrians were asleep inside their tents when they heard a scratching noise. When one went out to investigate, a bear immediately attacked him and carried him to an ice floe in the fjord as the others watched helplessly from a nearby glacier. Authorities later could find no traces of the victim or even his clothing.

It is hard, at first, to reconcile such ferocity with the easy amiability of the bears that came to visit us. Yet I recall that a year ago when ice left Hudson Bay in June, forcing the bears ashore early, most of them by October seemed lean and hungry, and one biologist who normally feels secure around them was alarmed as he watched them from the observation tower at Gordon Point, which is only a dozen feet above ground. The moment bears spotted him they tried to get him. That same fall, several shook the steel supports of my tower, two battering at the braces and looking up at me. I felt like the prophet Daniel in the lion's den. Bears were irritable that year. Before they would settle down to eat a tidbit below the tower, they would dash out again and again to scare away a fox that was simply watching. I didn't see a single bear engage in mock fighting.

So how dangerous a bear is depends in large part on how hungry he is. The bears at court in ancient times were undoubtedly well fed. So, too, are circus animals, who seem as tractable as big dogs. In fact, when the Norwegian explorer Roald Amundsen saw twenty-one bears in harness at the Hagenbeck Circus pulling a sled, he had an idea—why not use bears in place of dogs in exploration? He talked over the matter with the trainer, and after some experimentation, the two decided that just two bears were enough to pull a heavy sledge. However, at the last, the trainer declined to go along on the expedition, and Amundsen apparently didn't fancy handling the bears himself, so he went back to dogs, and much later went on to become the first man to reach the South Pole.

The most famous present-day polar bear trainer is a tiny blonde woman named Ursula Bottcher, and when she enters a cage crowded with ten big bears, the crowd grows silent, whether at Florida's Circus World or at Madison Square Garden. She is five feet tall and her bears tower above her: the biggest are eleven and a half feet tall and weigh sixteen hundred pounds. Her act is among the most arresting in the history of Ringling Brothers and Barnum & Bailey. Six males and four females overwhelm the cage as lions or tigers never do. They leap to their stands, jump through hoops of fire, and perform other acrobatics with a ponderous, teddy-bear charm. She waltzes with one, lets another take a sugar cube from her mouth.

Ursula comes from East Germany and started with lions. She prefers bears, which she considers much more intelligent than lions, as well as more dangerous. Her bears come from Russia as cubs, and beginning at ten months—never older—are trained to take their place on a particular seat in the cage, a place that remains theirs for the rest of their lives. She has worked with polar bears since 1964, and hers are presently between thirteen and fifteen years old. The females regularly have young, which she has been unable to keep alive.

Ursula says that her bears are most dangerous during mating season. It was then that the female Nixe knocked her down and, as she lay on the ground, tried biting her neck as all the other bears came off their stands and joined in the attack. Her assistant moved them back to their stands with a steel rod. "Maybe I was on the ground just seconds, but it seemed like hours. I moved, she tried to bite my neck—oh, it was terrible." She got up and continued her act. "I had to do the trick again. I had to dance with her right away. If I hadn't, then she would have known she was stronger than I."

It took thirty-five stitches to bind up Ursula's neck and shoulder wounds. She has an eight-inch scar on her right arm from the time a female scratched her. "She did it intentionally, without any reason. She wanted to do it. Of course, I finished the show, and then I went to the emergency hospital and they fixed it." A male during mating season entered the ring in a killing mood, tried sinking his teeth into her thigh, and, though he tore her tights from knee to hip, she escaped with no more than a scrape. Her secret for staying alive so far she says, is that she keeps them well fed.

In zoos, though popular with the public, polar bears are unpopular with zoo personnel. "They seem more aggressive toward keepers than the other bear species, and therefore more dangerous," says Mark S. Rich, curator of mammals at the San Diego Zoo. "Their temperaments vary from one to the next, but all are unpredictable," says Dennis W. Acus of the Cincinnati Zoo. Christian Wemmer, director of the Smithsonian's breeding farm for endangered animals, calls them "by far the most ferocious of all bears; other bears you can scare or bluff, but not the polar bear."

Hardly a summer passes without some child or even an adult climbing into the polar bear enclosure at a zoo. In Bloomington, Illinois, in 1969, when an eight-year-old boy "fell" into the pen, his grandfather jumped the fence, bopped the bear on the nose, grabbed his grandson, and climbed out. At the National Zoo in 1959, a boy "fell" over a barricade into the den of two bears and was being dragged toward their lair when an onlooker leaped in, drove off the animals with stones, grabbed the boy, and scrambled up a rope to safety. Seldom are the stories as pleasant as that; in Perth, Australia, in 1972, two bears mauled a young man to death. He had climbed a wire fence and dropped about twenty feet into a pool in the bear pit after scuffling outside with a number of men and a woman. Generally when someone is mauled at the zoo, the bear is promptly killed.

Can a bear that is fat and seemingly well fed be trusted when he comes up close? Isn't he perhaps looking for friendship? My questions betray my bias. For a long time I have been trying to prove to myself, at least, that bears are essentially friendly toward man.

During the fall of 1980, I had a chance to test my preconceived theories. At the invitation of a National Geographic movie crew, I crawled into a wire cage they had built for photographic purposes. They wanted to see how a bear reacts to a human suddenly thrust into their world, and I volunteered to test their response. The cage was four feet on each side with three-inch mesh, reinforced with angle iron. There isn't much room in an enclosure that small; it's about like trying to squeeze under a card table. Since I am six-foot-two and pretty wide, there wasn't much space left over. I had to keep my elbows tight to my body and my feet pulled up under me. I sat on a swivel seat just off the floor with a safety belt to keep me roughly in the center in case a bear might start rolling the cage over the tundra.

It took no bait to draw the polar bears to me; the odd-looking animal was curious enough. The first bear stopped short—surprised, shocked, incredulous. Then he approached cautiously. Others came up without a trace of hesitation. One started digging under the cage, like a dog after a ground squirrel. Another sat on his haunches and started pouncing at the wire, rocking the cage but not tipping it. One carefully inserted his jaws through the mesh, and tried clamping them together to crush the wire. When I tapped his nose he quickly withdrew and gave me what seemed like a hurt look, as if I had betrayed him.

One bear lay down and slowly reached his claws through the mesh to feel my boot. I pulled back and slowly put my boot on his toes. So for a few minutes we played footsie, a slow-motion game of covering toes with toes, to the vast amusement, it seemed, of the bear. Around the top of the walls of the cage was an aperture of six inches for photographic purposes, and some bears carefully inserted their paws a few inches and clawed gently at my parka. Those paws were enormous, armed with claws that were barely curved, black in young bears and brown in older ones.

There was no shortage of bears. At one time there were eight, with two more waiting their turn for a look. Their big black noses were wet and warm when I touched them with my fingers, even though snow was swirling around us at forty miles an hour. Frost kept forming on their eyelids, half covering their eyes. Periodically they would lift a big paw to try brushing it off. I tried helping them, without success.

I seemed enormously interesting to them. I can't believe that they mistook me for a seal or fox or dog, any of which they would probably have stalked or charged. There was no sign of hostility. They didn't seem to consider me a possible meal; rather, they seemed eager for companionship.

Never once did I feel endangered in any way, even though one big female crawled on top of the cage, so that all I could see above me was a cover of long white fur. Whether they would have eaten me, given the chance, I can't say. The previous year when most bears seemed hungry, the experience might have been quite different. And if I began to have delusions about their amiability now, they were quickly dispelled when a bear suddenly charged a colleague with a roar, ears laid back and long teeth flashing.

For the most part, however, the bears' fighting outside the cage was only play; they rose to their hind feet to box and feint and grapple and fall to the ground. Eventually their interest in me waned. Only one remained at the cage, lying at my feet dozing, as harmless, it seemed, as a family collie, and as lovable.

The trouble with being a polar bear, I thought as he lay there, is that everyone takes you seriously. When you're big and powerful and your paws are studded with claws like medieval instruments of torture, people flee, assuming you're out to eat them, even though at the moment you may be nothing more than curious. And curious is what you are always, for good reason. After roaming the ice for days of nothing but blinding white snow, the slightest change in color or form is bound to be exciting. So you move toward it, nose held high to catch the scent. You stop and lift yourself to your full height to get a better look. Then you drop down and move forward, sometimes at a run. So men fear you and from the beginning of time have fought you with dogs and spears and knives, and later, in their igloos, whiled away the long hours of night with stories of your strength, your wisdom, and your ferocity.

A Finnish biologist, Dr. Erik S. Nyholm, actually did make friends with polar bears, during two winters on Svalbard where he lived in a small hut among them. Supported usually by the University of Helsinki, Nyholm has studied polar bears for more than thirty years, during which time he has learned, as much as any man alive, their body language, their vocabulary of growls, hisses, chuffs, and roars, as well as their willingness to accept man into what he calls the society or community of bears. During the winter of 1968–69, he overwintered among the bears at Van Mikenfjord in southern Svalbard, along with a reindeer farmer and a master mechanic. During that time, Nyholm tranquilized and tagged bears. During the winter of 1971–72 at Nordaustlandet, he was denied a license to tranquilize and was enjoined by the Governor not to disturb bears in any way. His companions that winter were a wireless operator and a student. His only protection was a bear lance, a rifle, which he was instructed not to use, and three seasoned Karelian bear-dogs: Pima, Saida, and Lalli.

Nyholm describes that winter in the *Norwegian Polar Yearbook 1975–76:*

> On September 8, 1971, I saw the first polar bear near our station. After the 20th, bears were our regular guests as the enticing fragrance of seal spread itself downwind for as much as 30 kilometers. (Nearby walrus and reindeer interested bears very little.) The first bear, whom I named Rassari, was an old male who tried to plunder our supply of seal meat. At first he did little more than sleep. I found many daybeds nearby, including some with deep tunnels. After a week Rassari began to be dangerous, often trying to attack and paying little attention to shouts. But with my dogs and lance we managed to keep him under control. . . . To distinguish one bear from the next we marked them with waterproof ink that we applied on the end of a 1.5 meter stick. During October we marked nine bears. The last days in November when bear traffic

was lively, we had to be cautious when we took weather observations, snow depths, or did other work. The long winter passed without too much trouble except that bears broke two doors and eight window panes.

From my previous research I had come to recognize a bear's state of mind from his expression. An angry bear extends his upper lip. A friendly bear extends his lower lip, head raised, and moves with slow, heavy steps. An attacking bear moves with lowered head, light and soundless steps.

When we were working outside at night, my Karelian bear-dogs were our best life insurance. These dogs were accustomed to wild animals and ever prepared to do battle with them. Not a single bear could approach us or our station without our knowing it.

The 12th of October was a big day for us, for at 9:30 P.M. a big polar bear that we named Kalle [Finnish for Charley] came to the station. He was peaceful, and had just come up from the sea; masses of fat on his back and sides wiggled at each step. His beautiful glistening hide had no scar. He seemed to know there was seal blubber to be given out. I let him come within five meters. Here he stopped at my warning. I gave him some blubber. He seemed so friendly that I resolved to perform an experiment, to feed him from my hands.

I was amazed to see him beg for food in typical bear manner, which is to nod his head. I gave him many kilos from my hand; he didn't do the least thing to injure me. The distance between my fingers and his nose was barely 15 centimeters. When he sniffed my hand, holding a piece of blubber between his teeth, I wondered how much more he would sniff. I wasn't sure if I had pulled back my hand fast he would try to grab it. Kalle didn't smell how excited I was. He walked to a snowdrift to enjoy the wonderful blubber. After his meal, like all proper bears, he cleaned his fur, head and paws with snow.

Smell of blubber from our house carried some distance. We saw tracks of bears that came upwind, one from 20 kilometers. Bears didn't live at the station, but made long hunting trips. Kalle went about the houses in Kinnvika as he wanted. All the others kept away. Kalle stood highest in the social ladder, even though he was not the biggest or strongest. In encounters with others, his usual threat was a loud voice. Kalle's moves were lightning fast and his swats were effective. He knew the art of holding onto his dignity. We never saw him use his authority to take food from others—something that happens often between hungry bears of inferior rank. Judging from his condition, he must have been a really great seal-hunter. Many times we saw him leave a good part of his booty to other bears, not only to his closest friends.

Poorest of all in the art of hunting were two-year-olds that had left their mothers, and often begged food from good hunters. A young bear often follows an older one, and begs from it, moving right up to it. At first I thought this 'hunting pair' was a mother and young, until I found that often the big bear was a male. Two-year-olds Lulu and Lumu often tramped after Kalle, who was completely patient with them. They came as near as a meter before he gave a warning signal. When he was full, he allowed them to eat. Later the polar fox and gulls continued the feast.

Kalle was plainly interested in the females we had in the neighborhood, particularly Katrina and Maria. Even though they weren't in heat, he would follow their tracks a long ways.

A week after Kalle had come to Kinnvika, we had a visit from a new big bear that we called Iso-Antti [Big Andy], biggest of all at Nordaustlandet. I had seen his mighty tracks in the sand the day before, and was most interested in seeing how Kalle would receive the new giant. It happened on October 20. My notes follow:

At 5:45 P.M. I saw near the seal-house two big polar bears that lay and ate. They were Kalle and Iso-Antti. Lulu lay on one side looking hungry. Both big bears devoured seal blubber in harmony, and they licked one another's lips and throats as I often saw sister bears do. After eating, the big bears raised themselves on their back feet and slugged and prodded each other in fun. Iso-Antti went backwards five meters on his back feet. Then they were both down on all fours, but soon raised themselves again in full length, supporting themselves like heavyweight wrestlers. Kalle pushed Iso-Antti back again. There was an understanding between them when they rolled in the snow. All this took 14 minutes. Meanwhile, Lulu devoured the rest of the food.

(Bears can down a maximum of 39 kilos of pure seal blubber at one time.)

Later observations of these two big hunters suggested that Iso-Antti was inferior in rank to Kalle. Both resembled one another in appearance. It is possible they were brothers. If this assumption is true, it suggests that family relationship has meaning in the society of polar bears.

The two were the only ones that permitted me to follow them out on the ice to observe their hunting techniques. Kalle was swift both in locomotion and decision-making, yet had great patience when he hunted seals. Iso-Antti was slow, dull and reserved, but had great strength. Kalle liked to swim, but Iso-Antti often detoured nearly ten kilometers to avoid water.

When the friends ate kelp and algae, Kalle made a hole in the ice and dived in water 4 to 5 meters deep and brought up food. Iso-Antti stood by the hole and begged when Kalle brought up food. Both ate algae. Kalle lay in the water with front paws on the ice edge. Then Kalle would dive again after more. He kept doing this for 40 minutes, then pulled himself out, shook, and ate awhile, lying on the ice. Iso-Antti had by now had enough. What was left was eaten by other bears, especially Lulu and Lumu.

Kalle and Iso-Antti often walked together, Iso-Antti always lagging behind.

December was quiet in Kinnvika. All the bears lay buried in snowdrifts. The wind blew strong now and then, and the average temperature was −17.5°C, the lowest was −54.7°C. The seals, too, stayed under the snow. On some moonlight nights we saw frozen fog over Hinlopen Strait. In January the bears came again, and until July, when the last ice floes left, wandered to and fro. Spring was rich with food, for the fjords were full of young seals. New bears came along with our old acquaintances. My friendship with Kalle and Iso-Antti heightened my social standing among the bears. Their language of threats was blowing and mine was the speed of the snowscooter. My swats were rocks thrown at their paws.

It seemed certain that Nordaustlandet is a maternity denning area, since Katrina had two young, Manta had two young and Maria had one. We saw two females with young from a plane and one female with two young from a snowscooter at my favorite observation place, Nyholm Cape. Yet we found no maternity dens and realized that from the air it is almost impossible to differentiate a short-term one from a maternity den.

I proposed that Nordaustlandet be made a sanctuary. To my sorrow the Governor of Svalbard recommended that two hunters be given permission to shoot 20 bears. In vain I tried to prevent the hunting that would destroy the untouched condition of Nordaustlandet. One man shot ten big bears (the most profitable ones) and the other only one but thereby acquired a reputation for greatness. Shooting from the steps of a station needs little skill or courage. It is likely that Kalle, Iso-Antti and others met their death.

06

"The Finest Hunt
in the World"

A wild animal that will come up to men and even eat out of their hands—this is the creature that in the 1940s began to bring out hunters in airplanes. Generally two planes went out together, and when a bear was located, the plane with the hunter landed and the other drove the animal close enough to kill. The skin was taken as a trophy and the meat usually left on the ice.

Outdoor writers extolled the hunt. One wrote: "Kotzebue is still talking about the scores of trophy collectors who fly out over the arctic ice in their quest for big white bearskin rugs. As many as thirty planes were tied up on the ice waiting to carry out hunters."

Eskimos had been taking an average of 120 bears a year in Alaska during whaling, walrus, and seal hunting. Soon, sportsmen were taking twice that number. Hunting by plane was so simple that for the Eskimo, getting a bear no longer conferred any honor.

In 1957, the farthest from shore that a bear was taken in Alaska was sixty miles; the next year, it was two hundred miles. Many hunting parties said they saw the Siberian coast plainly and when they flew too close to the twelve-mile limit, radar screens on the American side were dotted with the blips of Russian interceptors. When hunters overflew Big Diomede, a Russian island separated by only three miles from American-owned Little Diomede, Soviet planes threatened seriously, alerting American jets.

Trophy hunting assumed alarming proportions. By 1965, outfitters were charging two thousand dollars for ten days of sport with a guarantee of a bag. Most customers were very rich Americans and a few wealthy Japanese. Some sportsmen took twenty shots to make their kill. A millionaire rancher from Mexico killed a giant bear after the plane landed on the Chukchi Sea just outside the border of the Soviet Union. Comparable hunting by Land Rover and tommy guns, the *Times* of London pointed out, had brought the Arabian oryx to the brink of extinction.

The *New York Times* chronicled polar bear hunts in Svalbard. A columnist told how American hunters watched with admiration as a big bear stalked a decoy seal near their ship. The bear was almost instantly aware of the dead seal but started out in the exact opposite direction, making a circle of a mile in and out of the water easing in "ever so gently with not a ripple." For the last hundred yards he swam, mostly underwater, and when he surfaced for the final charge, they shot him. He went into the water and came out again. Another shot and he dropped. Again he rose and ran a hundred yards before collapsing.

"The polar bear hunt off Svalbard," said the Norwegian Travel Service, "is one of the finest big game hunts in the world. Indeed, many big game hunters rate these bears over the grizzly, lion, or tiger. Hunting them among the pack ice is an experience that a hunter can never forget."

Two hunting groups from Norway, the *Washington Post* reported, killed four hundred bears, using snowmobiles and set-guns. Sealers in the Barents Sea and Denmark Strait killed an untold number more. In 1967, the Moscow biologist, Dr. Savva Uspenski, with considerable hyperbole, reported more hunters than polar bears in the arctic.

Even a century ago, conscientious people knew that no animal could withstand such slaughter. Admiral Peary on Franz Josef Island shot more than sixty bears in his first year, twenty-five in his second, and only twelve in his third. It would take only a few years, he wrote, "to kill out the species completely."

By 1965, the Russians reported that there were no more than five thousand to ten thousand polar bears left in the world. They begged other nations to help save polar bears from oblivion. Early in 1965, Senator E. L. Bartlett of Alaska called for an international meeting on polar bears. "I am informed," he said on the floor of Congress,

> that there are no accurate or reliable figures on the total world polar bear population or on the size of the annual kill. Scientists know very little about the habits of habitat, reproduction, longevity, or population structure. They do not even know the answer to the basic question of whether there is but one population of polar bears moving from nation to nation on the slowly revolving ice pack, or whether there are two or more populations. Are there Soviet bears and American bears, Danish bears and Canadian bears, or are there just the bears of the world? . . . I am determined to see that the polar bear does not follow the buffalo into extinction.

Shortly after, the *New York Times* came to the aid of bears, and in an editorial on 9 August, 1965 wrote:

> The polar bear is a victim of a peculiar—and particularly repulsive—expression of man's egotism. Wealthy men have taken to hunting bears in Alaska from airplanes. Two planes are used to herd the bear to an ice floe suitable for landing. While one plane lands and the hunter gets out, the other plane maneuvers the bemused animal within the hunter's gun sights. More than 300 polar bears, a new record, were killed in this fashion last winter in Alaska.
>
> This kind of hunt is about as sporting as machine-gunning a cow. Its only purpose is to obtain the bear's fur as a trophy for the floor or wall of someone's den. The carcass is left for scavengers.
>
> Norway and Alaska are the only places that actively encourage the degrading

"sport" as a tourist attraction. Russians do not hunt polar bears for sport and Canada forbids it by law, except by Eskimos.

On September 6, 1965, sixteen international official delegates met at College, Alaska, along with an assortment of U.S. bureaucrats and—to the dismay of the Soviets—observers from the Pentagon and State Department. Early in the meeting, the nonprofit Arctic Institute of North America made a proposal for a giant circumpolar research project lasting five years that would capture, tag, study, and fit polar bears with transmitters to be monitored by satellite. The Arctic Institute would be in charge. A U.S. Navy man spoke for the plan, but a Russian delegate saw sinister motives. Spokesmen for the plan kept silent for the rest of the conclave.

There was no agreement as to world bear population; a Russian scientist, Savva M. Uspenski, said eight thousand; the Canadian, Harington, said well over ten thousand. U.S. scientists said seventeen thousand to nineteen thousand.

There was a lively exchange of ideas concerning the polar bear. The Russian delegate questioned the widely held belief in the existence of subspecies. There were no "national" polar bear races or populations, but a common one, he said; a bear from Canada may some day appear in Greenland, Norway, Russia, or Alaska. Ice drifts, he said, cause mass movements of bears out of the Soviet Arctic to Norwegian waters and the Greenland Sea, then back to the Soviet, and this sweeping motion precludes formation of local races. The Canadian scientist, Harington, disagreed. He believed that bears stay near favorite hunting and denning areas rather than move in a stream around the pole.

Delegates totaled up the yearly bear kill: Canada, 600; Norway, 450; Alaska 300; Greenland, 100; Russia, 25; a total worldwide of 1,475. Attitudes towards hunting differed widely. Russia had completely outlawed all hunting of polar bears.[30] Canada forbade hunting by sportsmen but recognized the Eskimo's need for meat and skins. Greenland banned all hunting except by natives, most of them Eskimo. But in Norway, where sealing was a big industry, polar bears were considered predators and could be hunted all year round, by sealing crews, trappers, weather station personnel, and foreign tourists.

Deadly set-guns mounted in wooden boxes with baits were connected to triggers that would blast a bear in the face at point-blank range. One Norwegian hunter, Tromso's famous "Björnekonge," killed more than seven hundred. Bears were caught in traps, too, that were tended only in spring, since the dead bear was preserved by freezing.

Towards the end of the conference, Dr. Ivan A. Maksimov urged a five-year ban on all hunting, during which time denning areas would be mapped and permanent sanctuaries set up. The proposal met with silence. The following day he made another try. Still no response.

Russia's bears, said the Norwegian delegate, were indeed harvesting Norway's seals. Sanctuaries like the one his country had set up on King Karls Land was the way to go. Other delegates, too, had little interest in a total hunting ban. Hunting in the United States was big business, and since most animals killed were males, a total ban seemed unnecessary. No mention was made of the ethics of aerial hunting. Canada and Denmark saw no need for such a stringent measure; besides, their natives had long-standing rights to hunt.

The meeting concluded with no more than agreement that polar bears were an international circumpolar resource, that cubs and females with cubs should be protected at all times, and that the participating nations were to consider ways to promptly exchange information and to further research. In the next several years, however, polar bear specialists met at regular intervals.

When word went round that polar bears might soon become extinct, museum pieces only, the price of skins skyrocketed. Coral Harbour sent off thirty-seven skins during the winter of 1972 for an average price of $881; the next year, fifty-eight averaged $1,576 each. Pangnirtung, that picture-book village on Baffin Island, sent eight hides that averaged $884 in 1972 and four at $1,450 in 1973. Several hides late in 1973 sold for over $3,000 each, an increase of one-fourth over the previous year.

08

Research to
the Rescue

Hunting continued unabated. Early in the seventies, however, public resentment kindled. A quarter-page advertisement in the *New York Times* of June 27, 1971 read:

> Big, brave hunters are spending an average of $3,000 for the "privilege" of slaughtering one of the few remaining polar bears on this globe. They fly to Alaska, hire small aircraft and a guide, and blast away with high-powered rifles.
>
> We agree that everyone should have a polar bear "trophy" and we will send you one for only $15.00, thus saving you $2,985.00. Admittedly, our "trophy" isn't worth more than 25¢ as it is only a 1¼ inch button, but the other $14.75 will go to finance a knock-down, drag-out fight to save the polar bears, despite every effort of employees of the U.S. Government to "look the other way."
>
> Even Russia has prohibited the killing of polar bears—since 1957. But not our Department of the Interior or the Alaska Fish and Game Commission.

Concern for polar bears grew. Leading arctic scientists had already gathered in Morges, Switzerland at the headquarters of IUCN (International Union for the Conservation of Nature and Natural Resources) a world body formed in 1968. Delegates from the five polar bear nations met and reconvened at two-year intervals and, at Oslo on November 15, 1975, concluded with a worldwide agreement that hunting be banned except by local people using traditional methods.[31] Aircraft as well as large motor vessels were expressly outlawed. There would be no hunting where bears had not been taken by traditional means in the past. This in effect, created a sanctuary in the central arctic basin, but did allow some hunting by local people (in other words, mostly Eskimos and Indians) to be regulated by the country involved. The agreement, signed in 1973, did not take effect until May 1976, when three countries had ratified it.

Norway had already declared a five-year moratorium on all hunting and set up three national parks and two nature reserves comprising more than a third of all Svalbard, in which no trapping and no aircraft were allowed, and no hunting except for ptarmigan. Polar bears could be killed only in self-defense at weather stations and sealing areas.

Canada's quota system permitted a kill by Eskimos of 680 bears, each village given a set number of licenses. My friend, Wayne Born, a missionary-educator, was living among the Eskimos at Holman Island, a settlement of 230 on the west coast of Victoria Island, when word came that Canada was imposing a quota system. Holman Eskimos, among the most successful bear hunters, took the news philosophically and only commented that it wouldn't be long before bears would turn cannibal and start eating one another, because there were so many bears. Holman was given a quota of 12 bears. "They asked me to keep the licenses," says Wayne. "They didn't want a bear to know they carried in their pocket a permit to kill him. Each time they got one they came in and I wrote out a license. They got 13 that year, and ever since have tried to stay within their quota, which is now 20 bears."

Russia continued its ban on hunting and permitted only a limited number of cubs to be taken for zoos. Alaska had protected females with cubs for many years, and in 1972, the state outlawed use of aircraft for hunting. Just six months later, the U.S. Congress passed the Marine Mammal Protection Act, which forbade taking any polar bears (or walrus, sea otter, whales, seals, manatee, or dugong). Ever since, Alaska has been trying to regain control of its polar bears.

The world spotlight on polar bears gave biologists more funds for research. Their most immediate need, they felt, was a census of national and world populations. Next, it was important that animals be examined closely for disease, parasites, nutritional status, and overall health. To help determine seasonal and annual migrations as well as longevity and reproductive success, they must be marked and recaptured in specific areas over a period of several years.

The first biologists set out in 1966 in Alaska, Canada, and Norway's Spitzbergen with tranquilizing guns, ear tags, tattooing ink, and scales. The job, especially at the start, was dangerous. One scientist and his colleague set off in the dusk to follow a bear that had been tranquilized. They tracked it, using a flashlight, and wondered why it didn't collapse. When they found the tracks of a second bear, they slowly realized they had been following an undarted bear.

Among the early people who tagged bears was Charles Jonkel. At the start, it was hard to estimate the proper tranquilizing dosage, and, since the drug affects the muscles, several bears stopped breathing, requiring immediate artificial respiration. Fred Bruemmer tells of helping the crew in these emergencies. A man would lift the bear's front-quarters, then compress them six to ten times a minute. Lifting a big bear was a man-sized job, and one person would spell off the next after fifteen minutes. Seven bears that had stopped breathing all were saved, one after three hours of work.

Slowly, biologists perfected their techniques. Even so, it took courage, plus a sense of timing, precision shooting, and meticulous attention to details of both sanitation and safety. Other countries started tagging, too, using the skills developed by Canadians and Americans.

Denmark had started tagging in Greenland in 1973. A crew of biologists arrived with snowmobiles, two planes, and a sled dog named Rasmus, who was to distract a bear until it could be tranquilized. On the very first try, Rasmus, despite urging from the men, watched with indifference as two bears galloped into the mountains and escaped. So Rasmus was sent home on the next plane. Eventually the crew settled on a system. Pilots would spot bears, then either radio or drop a quickly sketched map to those on the ground, who would set out in pursuit, generally one man to a snowmobile. The rides were neither easy nor safe; sometimes the snow was soft, sometimes rock-hard. Bears generally ran from the snowmobile, moving fast on hard snow, dodging drifts and boulders, but floundering in soft snow. Surrounding the best areas were mountains towering nearly a mile above the ice. A bear at a distance from mountains or icebergs could sometimes be swerved away by plane or snow machine, but nothing could deter him when he got nearer to escape. If a bear did take cover in a small iceberg, men took after it with ice axes and ropes. Occasionally there were females in heat with one or two suitors, in which case the females were tranquilized first, since the males stayed nearby and could be captured later.

A bear was circled by machine until it tired and faced them within fifty or seventy-five feet. A cardinal rule of safety was that pursuers must move parallel, never behind an animal in case it should suddenly turn and attack. One bear, more exhausted than tranquilized, spun around at the touch of a stick and attacked, but collapsed before doing any harm. The snowmobiles performed without a single failure, and in two months the expedition marked twenty-four bears. The cost per bear was $3,700.

The following year, a helicopter eased this operation. Helicopters have greatly simplified the work of researchers, and in one day, as many as twenty bears can be tagged. Any of several tranquilizing drugs, fired into the neck or rear quarters, soon immobilizes a bear. Quickly, then, the bear is weighed with a scale supported by a tripod, or his girth measured which gives a good estimate of his weight; a blood sample is taken, and a non-functional tooth extracted. The tooth, decalcified in a mild hydrochloric acid solution until it feels rubbery, is washed, sliced, and stained, and cross-sections are made to examine the annular rings, which are a reliable indicator of age. A swatch of fur is chipped for an analysis of mercury content. His lip is tattooed for identification, and one or two tags are affixed to the ears. In a couple of hours, the bear begins to recover from the sedative, and, after a groggy beginning, he moves off to sleep away any lingering effects.

Bears are also snared for tagging. A V-shaped barricade of logs is set up and baited with a small cube of blubber; the trigger sets off a spring that boosts a wire cable up around the bear's paw. None of the bears we assisted in trapping seemed to suffer any ill effects.

Lentfer in 1977 was the first to begin fitting bears with radio transmitters to track their migrations by satellite. His first attempts, using three adult females, gave surprisingly diverse results. One female outfitted in March near Point Barrow moved straight north about 30 miles, where she was joined by a larger bear, probably a male. A couple of days later, she was located near a seal kill, after which the transmitter's signal failed. The second female traveled east against the direction of moving ice, and, when the signal failed three weeks later, she had gone 225 miles. The third, outfitted in June, traveled east for ten days, then moved west toward the Russian border. From mid-November to mid-April she moved very little; she may have denned on the ice and the movement was only that of shifting ice. The Russians tried locating her but were unsuccessful. In 394 days of tracking by satellite, she had moved nearly 1,000 miles.

Transmitter collars would not stay on the male polar bears; their neck and head diameters are too much alike. So the collars were kept in place by a body harness. After no more than a day, bears appeared to forget their harness.

Besides basic research, considerable applied research is going on, to develop safe means of repelling bears. This research is funded by branches of the Canadian government and by oil companies. A principal researcher in bear control is a young Canadian, Don Wooldridge, who has a background in engineering as well as wildlife. Oil companies asked Wooldridge to safeguard both men and bears on their offshore drilling islands.

Guard dogs were an obvious solution, except that bears approach from down-wind, undetectable to the keenest canine nose. Eskimo hunters were hired as watchmen; they were effective in daylight, but most drilling is done in the winter, when there are long periods without any daylight. Fences, too, were ineffective; a single night of drifting snow and they disappeared. Fires were useless. The age-old dictum that bears are afraid of fire and that a man is safe outdoors as long as he keeps a fire going is pure folklore. At the Churchill dump bears feed alongside big fires, seemingly immune to heat and smoke. To extract some tidbit, they often reach right into the flames, singeing their hair.

Wooldridge tried playing the recorded sounds of aggressive bears to repel approaching animals.[32] His first trial was at the Churchill dump in the fall of 1976, where a mother and cub were feeding. He recorded the results with a movie camera. The moment he turned on the recorder, both bears stood on their hind legs, the cub ran off at the sound but the mother appeared to take little action—except that she seemed to be getting bigger in the viewfinder. Suddenly Wool-dridge realized that the female was charging him head-on. He had time only to pick up his equipment, jump into the truck and turn off the sound as the female came full tilt up to the vehicle, brushed it a little as she smacked her lips in defiance, then moved off.

The human voice was completely ineffective at scaring bears. Big, fat Henry (named for Henry VIII) was a droll, amiable bear that spent a couple of weeks around the observation tower at Churchill. When Don turned on the speaker, Henry walked up to it, stood up and put both paws beside it, and looked in. Then at the sound of the recorded voice saying, "Get away, bear!" he bashed the speaker off its moorings. Loud sounds—like that of a boat horn—were equally ineffective.

The tower at Gordon Point east of Churchill, where Wooldridge had done much of his research, rises no more than twelve feet above the tundra, with two flights of stairs leading up to a somewhat flimsy crow's nest nine feet square, with walls of windows surrounded by an observation deck. The whole structure is lashed to the tundra by four cables, one of which was missing in 1977, when Don spent the fall there, most of the time alone. Northwest winds sweeping off the bay at speeds up to sixty miles an hour seemed to shake the cabin apart. A curious bear was halfway up the first flight of stairs before Don noticed it and fired a shot that frightened it down. He quickly equipped the stairs with a "red alert" trip wire.

At night Don always returned to Churchill in his pickup, but towards the end of his first season of testing, the snow piled up, making travel difficult. He decided to spend one night in his camper, which he had built out of three-quarter inch plywood, heavily reinforced to withstand bear damage. After a meal of chicken, he had just dropped off to sleep when the camper started to shake. He shone a flashlight at the window; a bear was peering in, a big paw on either side of the glass. It left, but ten minutes later, the front end of the truck dipped. Don found a pot and banged it against the wall, and for the next half hour he listened, wondering whether his plywood fortress was equal to the tremendous power of a polar bear. As he lay there, he heard the tailgate creak. A bear was probably going to test his back door, and though the latch was strong, Don picked up his .44 and waited. When there was no further sound for a few minutes, he opened the door and shone his flashlight out over the area. Within three hundred yards of his truck he saw not one but fifteen bears! He jumped to the ground, sped round to the cab, and drove back to town.

Don's preoccupation with his equipment, plus his need to be close to bears for his experiments, has given him some anxious moments. Early in his research he was getting out of his car at the Churchill incinerator. He had looked about the area carefully, but even the most careful scrutiny will not reveal a bear lying covered after a snowfall. Suddenly a bear came towards him, slinking, head lowered, obviously aggressive. Don grabbed the handle of the passenger door but found it locked. While he walked around the front, the bear walked around the back; he got in safely, but ever since he has been careful to leave all doors unlocked.

Probably few other safety engineers have involved themselves so personally or undergone more harrowing tests than Wooldridge has, but he does not deliberately expose himself, nor does he think of himself as a hero. Rather, he considers his dangers to be errors in judgment.

His nearest approach to oblivion came in the fall of 1978. He and a graduate student, Gary Miller, wondered to what extent a bear could be bluffed. It was anything but a scientific experiment that they tried one day on Sure (scar-under-right-eye), a troublesome young male. With guns they approached in short rushes, hissing and growling. Sure retreated. The two men spread out and approached from opposite sides, a maneuver that made the bear even more uneasy. Still, there was no headlong flight and soon the men stopped stalking the bear.

Not long after, Don was alone at the tower one afternoon. A bear had broken

The polar bear, revered and feared by the Eskimos, gave them clothing and food. He probably taught them how to hunt seals. Bear and man have surprising similarities.

Bruce Mikitok of Coral Harbour. The day before this photograph was taken, he used the spear to get a walrus at a nearby polynya. He has speared three bears.

Rosa Konayok of Repulse Bay, barely five feet tall, longs for the days when she hunted caribou and bears. She shot one bear when it started to enter her tent.

Timothy Lennie, famous bear hunter of Holman Island, on a hunt in a forbidden land where a lost tribe of "little people" lived in houses made of stone slabs.

Before the days of snowmobiles and planes, killing a bear was a mark of manhood. After the hunt, Eskimos honored the bear's spirit with a ceremony several days long.

Few acts in circus history equal Ursula Bottcher and her bears. A tiny German, she has been mauled several times. Her biggest bear stands eleven-and-a-half-feet tall.

Chicago's Brookfield Zoo brings off cubs, as do a few others. But too many zoos are miserable jails, whose crowded quarters turn bears into hopeless neurotics.

The big white skins have been prized since antiquity. They have sold for \$2,000 and more.

Kalle, a big male on Svalbard, looks in on Eric Nyholm, who spent the winter with him, even going along on seal hunts.

one of the trip wires that surrounded his bait. He descended the tower and looked all about carefully before he laid down his shotgun and crouched to splice the wire with his pliers. Moments later, to his left, he heard the snow crunch. Off no more than seventy-five feet in a fringe of willows was a bear stalking him, exactly the way a cat approaches a bird, pulling itself forward on its belly. Don reached for his shotgun at the same time the bear—seeing he was observed—charged full tilt. The first shot hit the ground when the bear was five feet away. The bear whirled but was not about to retreat until a second shot caught it in the rear quarter. Don wondered why the bear didn't go down but fled, limping. Then he remembered that he had been hunting ptarmigan the previous day and hadn't replaced the bird shot with the slugs he normally carried.

The next day when we talked to him, Don was still somewhat shaken, but concerned more about the bear—which turned out to be Sure—than his own split-second escape. He notified conservation officers and wrote a detailed report, required of anyone who shoots a bear. Two days later when Don took us out over the desolate tundra to the tower, a bear was waiting at the base next to the stairway. It was Sure, and to Don's pleasure, it moved away without the trace of a limp.

There was no hint of vindictiveness as Don watched the animal which—except for the sound of the snow crust—would almost certainly have killed him. Instead, he was apologetic. "Without that taunting we did a few days ago," he said, "he might have behaved quite differently. He saw me alone and unobserved, and his familiarity with us had lessened his fear. So he decided to strike." In Don, there is a strong element of kismet, of a divine plan. "If I hadn't forgotten to change to shotgun slugs, either the bear or I would have been dead. This way we're both alive."

Wooldridge's continuing work with acoustics is meeting with mixed results. In the first year, nine bears were repelled 100 percent of the time by aggressive bear sounds; in the second year, seven bears were repelled only 35 percent of the time. A composite synthesis of aggressive bear sounds doubled the effectiveness. Unfortunately, though, a bear must first be seen and allowed to approach closely before the noise is effective. At a drill rig in the Beaufort Sea, Don installed a sound system. Shortly after he left, a bear approached, and, when it was still six hundred yards away, the recorded roars were beamed at it unsuccessfully. Later it returned and at one hundred yards—the proper distance—the machine was turned on, scaring it off.

Trip wires that activate warning buzzers have proved workable but there are problems. Foxes can set them off. So too can dogs. Men stumble into them. The result is that warning sounds are not always taken seriously. More than that, drifting snow limits the reliability.

An electrified fence has been only marginally successful. The problem is that a bear's long hair effectively insulates against anything other than a dangerous voltage. Animals that touched their noses to the wire or were otherwise shocked were effectively conditioned, perhaps for a long time.

Still another warning device Don has tried is a proximity antenna, which functions when the animal gets near. In his first year's trials, some 63 percent of forty-one approaches were detected. His current project is the use of laser beams mounted on posts at each corner of a drill site. A beam intercepting the bear would signal a warning, but there are problems here too. A blizzard might contain enough snow to break the beam; posts at the corners might move with shifting ice, pushing the receptors out of range. Despite the drawbacks, the system seems promising and should be able to reach out into the winter dark.

Wooldridge will also try low-frequency or subsonic sounds that presumably would cause discomfort to bears, along with high-density, infra-high sounds.[33] In fact, he is not averse to trying any idea proffered him, from a mock bear with speaker inside to a speaker-equipped mannequin that would pop up as a bear approaches.

So far, almost every repellent and warning system works—part or even most of the time. "But obviously that isn't good enough," says Wooldridge. "What we offer must be 100 percent effective, and we haven't figured that out yet." In the meantime, he will provide a redundancy of systems, and oil companies will probably continue to hire Eskimos to patrol drilling areas.

During the fall of 1979, Don and Scott Mair were in the Gordon Point tower, keeping quiet and motionless so as not to alert the animals below them. One bear looked up and either saw or smelled them and started running around the base of the tower in a frenzy. Then it found the stairway, climbed over a plywood barricade, and started up. Don fired a shot above the bear's head, but it kept coming. He fired a second shot without effect. Scott lobbed a thunder-flash at it. By now the bear was on the landing, starting up the second flight. In another ten steps he would have been at the flimsy door and a single swipe could bash it in. The bear crouched like a cat moving on a mouse, and moved up. Don could do nothing but fire directly at him with his revolver, flipping off one shot after another, until the fourth shot started the bear backing down. Finally, he leaped over the barricade and ran off across the lake, seemingly uninjured.

It might seem surprising that Wooldridge is an exponent of the rights of polar bears, but he explains, "Does man have the right to come to the arctic and say, 'Good. Look at all the possibilities here. Of course we'll have to get rid of bears and make the place habitable'? It is the ultimate conceit to say 'Let's blast away the bears; this land belongs to us.' "

The Town That Loves
Polar Bears

Churchill, Manitoba, is a village of sixteen hundred perched atop a ridge of low, rounded rocks on the western shore of Hudson Bay. It is the end of the line for a railroad that brings wheat from the Canadian prairies to be loaded onto ships bound for Europe. Cape Churchill, forty miles east of town, is the end of the line for an age-old polar bear migration route, as the bears come there every summer from two or three hundred miles farther south down the coastline. The situation is incredible: a town on the migration route of one of the world's most dangerous carnivores.

Churchill is subject to continuing danger from bears for three months of the year, one year after another. Yet the human inhabitants love their bears. Churchill is a remarkable example of how man and a dangerous animal can coexist. Only in the last dozen years have bears been a serious problem there, even though the town dates from 1771, when a fort (the most northerly in America) was built to guard the mouth of the river. Bears that used to wander into town were simply shot as food for sled-dogs and their hides sold for a few dollars.

World War II brought a U.S. Strategic Air Command base four miles east of town, and for American GIs, polar bear skins became a prize to be smuggled back home. Bears were so scarce then that one day, when a big one came to town, men stopped work, women came out of their kitchens, and crowds took out after him until he found refuge under the floor of the lumberyard. Mothers who called to their children to keep back stood in the front row themselves. Thunder-flashes only made him growl. Then someone called for the fire hose. "That'll get him out for sure," people said. But when the stream of cold water reached him, the big bear loved it and stretched out in great enjoyment. He stayed under the shed for three days and then left one night on his own.

Since then, for several reasons, the numbers have grown. During winter, bears strike out north and east over the ice for a hundred miles or more to hunt, but constant north winds and current keep moving the pack ice south, and along with it, the bears. As the ice melts during summer, the last of it hangs up on the shallow flats on the southwest rim of the bay, and this is where in July bears are forced ashore. A few move inland, but most start migrating north for a remarkable

111

reason. Bears seem to know or somehow sense that ice—which means seals and a resumption of hunting—forms two and even three weeks earlier at Churchill than elsewhere because of dense freshwater ice that forms in the broad river and is discharged into the salty waters of the bay.

From September and well into November, polar bears walk the streets of Churchill at any hour of the day or night, sometimes followed by children and dogs and picture-takers, and taxing the efforts of conservation officers and Mounties to keep them out. At the Legion Hall, a bear walked in at midday and proceeded toward a crowd of dart throwers until the club steward, an old English army major, saw him and shouted, "You're not a member. Get out!" The bear left.

An airline agent and his family were sitting down to dinner in their summer cabin when a bear leaped through the picture window and started to help himself. The agent beat the bear out of the house with a two-by-four.

Gilbert Jordan had just cooked a big roast. He left the house long enough for a bear to enter and finish the feast. He shot the bear in his living room.

At the Harbour Board kitchen, a bear walked past a bag of pork chops and went off with a bag of garbage.

One Churchill man figured to make it big in the hog business, using garbage from the air base. But as soon as the bears came to town, they polished off every pig, and for the next several years, remembering that bonanza, returned looking for more.

While the family was at a school concert in 1976, a bear pushed through the screen door of the Godwin Phillips trailer home and licked the butter dish clean, finished off the leftover chicken, tore off a piece of paneling, and left before the family came home.

Some twenty snowmobiles were parked outside the summer cabins at Camp Nanook, near town. In the morning, hardly a machine still had its plastic seat intact. (Bears seem to love the taste of plastic.)

A British pilot was leaving the Arctic Inn to make an early-morning flight. In the narrow entryway sat a polar bear. "Not the thing a chap ordinarily encounters on his way to work," he told the motel owner. By the time his copilot came, the bear was gone.

The night watchman at the Satellite Launch Center heard the sound of steps in the office upstairs, even though the building was locked and everyone gone. When he crept upstairs he met a bear—face to face—that had entered by a fire escape. It ran off.

Moe Bellerive, a voluble French Canadian, was making repairs to his summer cabin at Goose Creek, south of town, when he spotted a big, gaunt polar bear sniffing at the doors of nearby cabins. A stone's throw from his door was an aging phone booth, its door long gone, and Moe hurried to it. With his first dime, he reached his wife. Just as he heard her answer, he was suddenly aware of two things: that he lacked a second dime to complete the call, and that the bear was just outside, eyeing him closely. "Hello, hello, hello," he could hear his wife say, and then with exasperation, "Another wrong number!" as she hung up. His dime returned, he reached the operator, who summoned the Mounties to rescue Moe from his precarious refuge.

Maurice Morand, a trapper at Goose Creek, had made a fish stew for supper and put the leftovers on his screened porch to freeze. Around 2:00 A.M. he heard a rattling sound but concluded it was the wind and went back to sleep. A little later there were loud bangs. He dressed to go outside, but got no further than the glass door. Just outside on the porch was a bear eyeing him intently and ready to enter. Maurice's cabin has no attic, no basement, and no door between living room and bedroom. There was no safe place to go. His guns were in another cabin, but he didn't dare risk jumping out a side window. The highest place inside was his kitchen cabinet just inside the door, and that is where he went and sat, eyes glued to the bear, which eventually sat down and much later fell asleep. "For three hours I sat there," said Maurice, "while the bear slept." Finally, the bear got to its feet and left; after it was well outside, Maurice lobbed a thunder-flash to frighten it further off, but that didn't work. Then he pounded two pie plates together; the bear ran and never came back.

In August 1980, Bill Clifford, flying his helicopter back to Churchill, ran out of daylight and stopped at an air strip at Seal River, where he saw two planes parked. The cabin he knew would be occupied so he walked over to one of the planes and crawled in. Past midnight, in the moonlight he saw a bear approach his helicopter and smash the bubble, then claw through the door and start ripping away the plastic seat cover. Then the bear came to the plane Bill was in, and began pounding away at the fuselage, pushing the side in a good three inches. Then the bear climbed onto the fuselage and looked in the back window, but for some reason didn't smash it. Instead he continued pounding at intervals until morning, when the two pilots chased the bear off with a few blasts of a shotgun.

Such are the stories that liven the morning coffee hour at the airport and down at the harbor. Some come from earlier days. Dutch Pete, a trapper so big he seemed like a bear himself, was inside his tent along the Churchill River in 1936 when a bear tried to get inside. Pete grabbed an ax and split its head open. John Ingebrigtson's mother, a tiny woman from Norway, was home alone when she heard a noise on the porch. She muttered to herself that the children must have left the door open. When she saw it was a bear she grabbed her broom and whacked it on the rear, scaring it off. "Not too many things can stand up to a woman with a broom," says John.

Not all encounters are comic. A seven-year-old boy on his way to Sunday School met a bear coming around a building and did exactly what he had long been instructed to do: drop to the ground and play dead. The bear tipped him over and then went on.

In 1966 a subadult male attacked a twelve-year-old boy but was shot, and the following year, another subadult male knocked down a Chipewyan woman who was carrying home her groceries; a Chipewyan boy shot it. The year after that a nineteen-year-old Eskimo boy was killed by a bear. He and two friends had found a bear track near the school grounds. They took the track, following fast for only a short way, then met another track, where the victim separated from his friends. In dropping over a large boulder, the boy jumped almost on top of the bear, which was sleeping under the branches of a tree. This has been the only fatality from a bear at Churchill.

Jonkel autopsied the three bears involved. The bear that had attacked the boy in 1966 had been shot earlier in the year, and the shot had driven a canine tooth into the nasal passage and blinded one eye. Earlier the same day it had been shot with a .22 in the abdomen and hind legs. The bear that attacked the woman had been captured and ear-tagged ten days earlier, and for the previous two months had lived at the dump, where it had been photographed, fed, and chased with cars until it had little fear of men. The bear that killed the young Eskimo had given no earlier indication of being dangerous, but its attack could hardly be called unprovoked.

Nearly always it is food that prompts a bear's attack. Perhaps the woman should have let go of her groceries, some people said, instead of hanging on to them. Certainly the British Broadcasting Corporation crew whose car stalled at the incinerator should have thrown out their lunch. Don Wooldridge was waiting for the car to leave before he started his research. As he watched, he saw the bears exploring every door and window. After fifteen minutes, he studied the car with his field glasses and saw that the occupants were signalling to him frantically, beckoning him to come. Their car was stalled.

But Don's truck didn't frighten the bears away, even though he nudged one of them with his bumper. The horn made no difference, nor did his acoustical devices. Finally he angled his truck alongside the car so their bumpers met, opened his passenger door to meet the opened door of the driver's side and, in the dubious shelter of the door-enclosed triangle, pulled the British crew into his cab and drove off. From a distance they watched what happened next. No more than one minute later, a bear climbed onto the hood and pounced on the windshield, smashing it against a movie camera. With one sweep of his paw he hurled the camera backward with such force that it cracked the rear window. What the camera crew hadn't realized was that the smell of their lunch was drawing the bears in.

A mother separated from her cubs is dangerous, too. Eric (Red) Euteneir, an airline employee, will never forget the Saturday night of November 19, 1977. He told me exactly what happened.

> I was guiding in a YS11 and ran out of the hangar door onto the ramp, flashlight in hand. I wondered why the pilot kept his landing lights on—usually he shuts them off at that point. He kept coming, revving his engines as I kept backing up. Then for some reason I looked behind me. I saw a polar bear not more than five feet away. I shone my light at it because I couldn't believe my eyes. Sure enough, it was a bear. She stood up on her hind legs and growled. I started running towards the plane, thinking the roar of the engines would scare her, but she kept chasing me. I slipped on the ice but got up

again. The bear kept coming. I ran toward the hangar, and at that point the pilot applied power again. Now I had to avoid the plane as well as the bear. I ran to the hangar and got safely inside. If it hadn't been for the quick thinking of the pilot, I wouldn't be alive today. Later he told me the bear swiped at me just as I slipped and fell out of reach. Don't ask me how I felt because I don't know how I felt.

The bear had lost sight of her two cubs and was desperate.

Trappers are the most likely candidates for bear troubles, and indeed, old Jimmy Spence, whose nephew lost his arm to a bear, said, "It was better years ago when we shot them for dog food." Most trappers, however, disagree. Joe Kowal says, "I can't say anything bad about them. They set off a few of my traps now and then, but I can't complain." He tells how occasionally when he is out hunting geese, a bear may saunter over to pick up a downed bird. Joe simply leaves without an argument. " 'So you want to hunt here,' I tell him, 'I'll find another place.' "

Property damage to summer homes and hunting lodges from bears is high. Six miles east of town is a lake fringed with a few stunted spruces where local residents have built a line of cabins. The place is appropriately called Camp Nanook. A drive down the street in the fall reveals an array of boarded-up windows and doors and a general look of abandonment. Shutters are no insurance against damage. One bear clawed and bit its way through three-quarter inch plywood to get at some caribou meat stored for a pack of sled dogs, then ate one of the dogs.

Of the twenty-two cabins at Camp Nanook, nineteen were broken into during the fall of 1978, possibly by the same she-bear and cub. One cabin she didn't bother belongs to Boris Oszurkiewicz. Below the door and every window he set four-by-five-foot panels of planks bristling with eight-inch spikes set at two-inch intervals. Except for one bear so tall that it reached across the panel and smashed a window, Boris has had no bear trouble. One morning, however, forgetting his own barricade, he walked out of the door and landed in the hospital.

Churchill is determined that bears and people can get along, and to that end there are slide shows and lectures on bear safety at school, public service announcements, telephone recordings by the Mounties, and garbage bags of all sizes. Phone directories list bear-alert numbers. The crucial night of the year is Halloween. To safeguard trick-or-treaters, volunteers ring the entire town in cars with short-wave radios and flashing lights, and every porch light in town is turned on.

Garbage remains the major problem, luring bears into town. A few years ago an incinerator was installed to burn all garbage, but bears barricaded the entryway for trucks, climbed in and out of a small hatch designed for after-hours disposal, and several times kept trash collectors up steel ladders until help arrived. Currently the incinerator is out of operation.

Conservation officers work with the Mounties to protect the community and, as far as possible, the bears. During fall, reinforcements from elsewhere in Manitoba help man the twenty-four-hour alert. Most of these young men are conscientious, but one with a swagger earned the nickname of "Speedy" for the prompt way he killed bears. When an animal was surrounded by onlookers and had no place to run, he would shoot it on the spot. After a season he was transferred.

The daily bear activity sheet kept in the conservation office, beginning some years as early as June, reads like a police blotter.

10:30 A.M.	Behind complex, 1 reported lying in rocks, not seen.
2:45 P.M.	Flats, 1 bear in empty shack. Chased out and down river. Set trap.
4:10 P.M.	Flats, 2 sighted in rocks.
6:00 P.M.	Flats, 1 chased by cops
6.45 P.M.	Flats, 1 chased out again
8:15 P.M.	Flats, 1 chased away from Erik Carlson's
10:30 P.M.	Superior St. 1 couldn't find
11:30 P.M.	Flats, 1 seen but couldn't find again

A woman phoned that a bear was knocking at her door. The Mounties sped to the spot with a searchlight and routed it. On the heels of that call came one from the Flats. When the Mounties came near an abandoned building, a small bear came to the window to look out, seeming to greet them.

"How do you dare live in a town full of polar bears?" a television cameraman asked Penny Rawlings of the Arctic Inn. She countered, "How do you dare live in New York where you run the chance of being mugged? Like you, we simply know what places to avoid at night, and what to avoid during the day."

"Bears? We can live with them," says Ella Barron, who works at the Legion Hall. "I'm more scared of a pack of dogs, especially when trappers come into town in spring from a winter up the coast."

Bill Erickson's two-story home sits on a rock like a sentry tower east of town, and it is often the first stop for bears on their way in. During the fall of 1976, Bill chased seventeen bears out of his yard. How does he go out of the house at night? "Carefully," says Bill, "and I always lead with my eyeballs."

Visitors to town are full of solutions. Move the dump far inland, or better yet, move the town. Fence the town with high netting or electric wire. Fly bears away, and indeed this was done for a couple of years, transporting them south some 250 miles, at a cost of five hundred dollars per bear, paid for by the International Fund for Animal Welfare. Most of the bears stayed away, but three males came back in seventeen days, and a mother and her cubs returned in two weeks, the cubs somewhat heavier but the mother lighter by a hundred pounds. In 1981, a Quonset hut at the airport was fitted with twenty large cages to hold problem bears until freeze-up.

Despite the very real dangers from bears, most Churchill residents wouldn't have it otherwise. A doctor at the clinic observes, "Nothing unites the people of town as much as polar bears. We love them." Moe Bellerive says, "I've seen hundreds of bears, but never a belligerent one." And even though they helped themselves to his tame ducks and broke into his cabin, Moe says, "That was only once in fifteen years." Doug Webber comments, "I only wish they'd go out the same hole they came in." His goose-hunting cabins have been broken into six times

Flying over the denning area we saw a mother running, two cubs on her back. Dennis Andriashek, biologist, caught one that got separated from its mother.

He was twelve pounds of fury as Dennis brought him to the helicopter to search for his mother. Born four months before, he had weighed little more than a pound.

He soon quieted down and explored the cockpit. When he growled or hissed, Dennis responded in kind. They seemed to form an almost immediate bond.

As we searched for the mother, the cub kept watch out the window. When, after two hours, we found her, the cub seemed reluctant to leave us—a mutual feeling.

With the mother tranquilized, we weighed the cubs.

In March this cub, a single, weighed 55 pounds, the biggest ever recorded for one only four months old.

We stood watch as they slept, since for a few hours they were helpless against other predators. By the end of our stay, they were ready for their long march to the sea.

Many bears that come to the Churchill dump have never before seen or felt fire. Though their fur is singed, they still extract tidbits from the flames.

RIGHT:
If this yearling grows bolder and continues to prowl the town, he may need to be flown away—an expensive measure—confined until freezeup, or else shot.

As the arctic continues to be explored, his future is uncertain, and depends on the public.
Polar bears are a national and an international treasure.

in one winter. "Invariably," he says, "they break a new hole in the wall or window or door when they leave."

Now tourists are beginning to travel to Churchill on bear-watching tours. A few businessmen realize the potential in tourism, but for the most part Churchill simply likes its bears. To Americans looking for easy solutions, it must seem incredible not to exterminate a dangerous animal, the way California long ago systematically killed off its grizzlies. California, whose state symbol is a grizzly, once had a population of 155,000, but the last one was shot in 1922.

The grizzly has also disappeared from Oregon, and in Washington State only a few bears survive, one in the extreme northeast corner and perhaps one or two in the North Cascades National Park. The only grizzly populations of any size outside Alaska are an estimated six hundred to eight hundred in Glacier and Yellowstone National Parks.

British Columbia and Alaska have a total of perhaps thirty-five thousand grizzlies. Concerning this depletion, Aldo Leopold commented, "There seems to be a tacit understanding that if the grizzly survives in Canada and Alaska, that is good enough. It is not good enough for me. Relegating the grizzly to Alaska is like relegating happiness to heaven. One may never get there."

The people in the town of Churchill, Manitoba, have proved that man can live happily—though sometimes precariously—with nature, if he chooses to. Last time I lunched at the Churchill Café, I overheard someone say, "Bears were here long before people." The village council has no intention of eliminating polar bears, which add flavor, distinction, and excitement, something frontiersmen have always liked.

09

What About the Polar Bear's Future?

The *Red Data Book* of the International Union for the Conservation of Nature and Natural Resources now lists polar bears as "vulnerable," a status just above "endangered." Though polar bears are in no immediate danger of extinction, their numbers do need careful monitoring.

So too does the arctic environment; even a slight warming might prove hazardous. Disappearance of the ice cover, suggested as a possibility by the Russian scientist Budyko, would be catastrophic to seals and bears. The Danish specialist, Christian Vibe, points out that bears and ringed seals both need a stable climate without a winter melt in order to den successfully.

Too much ice can be disastrous, too. Severe icing in the Beaufort Sea during the winter of 1973 and again in 1974 caused the numbers of ringed and bearded seal to drop to half and their reproduction rate to only 10 percent; numbers and productivity of polar bears declined noticeably. If leads along the western arctic or Hudson Bay somehow froze over, the effect on marine animals would be devastating. Stirling says, in "Polynyas" in the *Canadian Arctic:*

> Local populations that depend on polynyas for their overwintering survival, such as the walruses and bearded seals in the area of Penny Strait and Queens Channel, would probably be eliminated. While we recognize that such major physical changes seem unlikely in the foreseeable future, the results might be similar if man's activities resulted in large-scale disruptions to polynyas or the lower organisms of the food chain that reside there.

Seals seem as limitless in numbers as buffalo must have appeared to the pioneers. In early summer, when seals lie on the ice scratching off their winter pelage, they seem to be everywhere, dotting the surface as far as you can see. But the scene is misleading—ringed seals stay mainly along the coast, feeding on bottom-dwelling invertebrates, as mentioned earlier, as well as on fish and, in deeper waters, on the top layers of crustaceans. Bearded seals, a secondary food source for bears, are even more creatures of shallow water, feeding on a wide variety of shrimps, crabs, hermit crabs, marine worms, mollusks, and bottom fish. Little is known about the productivity of these marine life forms or about the degree to which seals move in response to fluctuations in their food supply. The factors that limit ringed seal populations might be stable ice for pupping, or it might be food supply. Unlike the antarctic with its giant upwelling of nutrients and abundant marine life, arctic waters are generally unproductive of marine flora and fauna.

The arctic, with its limited diversity of animals, is often in severe imbalance. On land, the lemmings are a major source of food for foxes, snowy owls, and gyrfalcons, and when they are scarce, those predators suffer. In winter, foxes on the ice feed mainly on the remains of seal kills, so that a healthy population of bears is essential to the fox population.

Bears, with their almost complete dependence on a single food source, would be especially vulnerable to any major ecological change. Nils Øritsland of Norway, researching the energy requirements of bears, estimates that six hundred bears in the Hudson Bay area need a minimum of eight thousand seals during their eight months on the ice. A major oil spill could be a catastrophe to seals of an area. It would foul the hair of bears swimming in oil-covered water and destroy their food supply, and they might be damaged by ingesting oil as they lick themselves clean.

So what is to happen when drill rigs invade the polynyas, which are the habitat of migrating birds as well as seals, walrus, and narwhals and other whales? To start with, Stirling says in his brochure on polynyas, that

> the penchant of narwhals and white whales for entering small leads and patches of open water has been well documented, as has the regularity with which they become entrapped. Some biologists are concerned that whales may follow icebreakers away from the polynya areas during winter only to be trapped in unnatural patches of open water left in the wake of ships and subsequently perish.

Lentfer and Stirling both believe that the greatest danger for polar bears and their habitat is an increase in energy exploration and development, which has already begun and is pretty certain to continue. Lentfer believes that exploration around maternity dens might cause denning mothers to desert their dens too early. A seismographic crew early in March 1974 saw a female with a new cub traveling across the bay a month earlier than normal, possibly because of human activity in the area. Some bears are unconcerned, however; a female and two cubs during the same winter paid no attention to passing vehicles. (Here again is that divergence in behavior that makes generalizing so difficult.)

The oil industry has laid down strict rules to safeguard bears. Besides strict sanitation and a ban on personal firearms, no harassment by aircraft is permitted. Known denning areas are avoided. Oil spilled on snow or ice is easily recovered with heavy earth-moving equipment that has been field tested for the best techniques. Oil trapped in openings in the ice can be pumped into barges. The biggest problem would be oil that gets under the ice; fortunately, it doesn't spread fast. Gunter Weller of the U.S. Outer Continental Environmental Assessment Program says that the underside of sea ice is irregular, with many corduroylike concavities that retain oil floating on water. To remove it, engineers have developed what they call a rope mop skimmer. Two holes are cut in the ice and a rope is inserted, threaded through, and joined to form a loop around pulleys at each end. As the loop revolves, it picks up oil that is removed by a squeezing through a "skimmer" mounted on a barge or other vessel. Currently a big vessel with two hulls is being designed with a rope mop skimmer mounted between the hulls; it will operate in conjunction with a barge equipped with an incinerator to burn the oil.

More important than possible contamination is the effect of greatly stepped-up activity in the arctic in general. A Manitoba brochure sums up the danger:

> Drilling rigs have operated within a few miles of the denning site. With a railway on one side and potential oil wells on the other, the site is neither remote nor safe. There are other threats, among them an array of chemicals like PCB's and mercury carried down rivers into the bay, any of which could shrink the food supply for seals. And if the seals go, the bears go. Man's hand lies upon every white bear in the arctic, and indeed upon every living creature.

So far, the levels of chlorinated hydrocarbons, including the DDT group, hexachlorobenzene, dieldrin, and endrin, have been found to be at such low levels that they probably have a minimal effect, according to work done by Lentfer on bears killed in Alaska from 1967 through 1972. He suggests that new samples be checked periodically.

Because bears are such commanding, high-profile figures, they will continue to be political. Do the Russians supply bears that are killed in Alaska? There is evidence that they do, since few maternity dens have been discovered in Alaska, perhaps not enough to replenish those killed by natives. Russian bears travel to Norwegian waters, too, and there may soon be pressures to resume hunting on Svalbard. Currently, Norway has stopped set-gun and trophy hunting (since 1971), permitting bears to be killed only in self-defense. Denmark permits its Greenland Eskimos to hunt, but has outlawed set-guns, the use of snowmobiles, and the shooting of females with cubs.

Canada allows an annual kill of 680 bears, which most biologists agree is the very top limit that can be taken without diminishing the population. Eskimos and Indians are permitted licenses under a quota system allocated to villages. These licenses can be sold to white hunters, but generally are not, since hides continue to command high prices. The highest bidders at auctions are the Japanese, many of them farmers who have sold their land to urban developers and are suddenly rich, and though they may have no walls or floors big enough for a polar bear skin, they want the prestige that the skin confers.

Eskimos are confused by the wildlife regulations imposed on them. They want to control the polar bears, which they feel are theirs, and this might be possible were it not for pressures by white hunters, frantic to prove their courage and manliness. Andy Mumgark of Eskimo Point says:

> When God created man, Inuit and Qablunaat were each given their own land to care for. Inuit were born in the north, and northern wildlife became theirs to manage.

Today it is not we who make the wildlife regulations. The Fish and Wildlife officers have become the caretakers of our land. The animals no longer belong to us.

Both Lentfer and Stirling favor hunting where bear populations grow too dense for human safety or the bears' own food supply. There is value in hunting, they say. It keeps bears at a distance and maintains their natural (nongarbage) behavior.

Alaskans resent the federal takeover of their marine wildlife, including polar bears. They say the Marine Mammal Protection Act of 1972 gives no protection to mothers and cubs and places no limit on hunting by natives, either by numbers or by method. Under their old law, superceded by the federal law, any resident of Alaska could take three bears a year for subsistence, and mothers and cubs were protected.

Lentfer believes that polar bears can be hunted in limited numbers in Alaska without harm to the population, and is asking that jurisdiction over them be returned to the state. He advocates two kinds of hunting, one subsistence and one recreational. Any resident who needs a bear for food could take one per year without a permit, with the freedom to sell the skin. Recreational hunters could take one bear every four years by permit only. Open season for both kinds of hunting would extend from January through May. It seems to me, however, that whether or not to hunt polar bears—certainly a national treasure—is a question for more people than the residents of one state to decide.

Elbert Rice, head of engineering at the University of Alaska, has another suggestion: "Let anybody hunt bears, any time of the year and all year, providing only that he hunts in the traditional manner: no planes, no snowmobiles, and no guns, only with dogs and stone-tipped spears."

His suggestion is not to be taken lightly. Bear-hunting by plane and snow machine is a slaughter no real sportsman can stomach. Killing a bear that way takes no skill or courage. If you miss the first half dozen shots, you simply keep on shooting until the animal drops. No true hunter would countenance such a fraud. I know the hunting ethic because—though I no longer hunt—I did so for many years. A hunt, first of all, should be just that: a search where skill and knowledge of the animal's habits are essential. Next, it must be a sport, where animals get a sporting chance to escape. And if the hunt calls for endurance and courage, so much the better.

Animals that are regularly hunted must learn fear if they are to coexist with man, and this is what I dislike most about a return to hunting. Fear is an ugly thing to see. Animals that cringe or race away are clumsy, awkward, inviting contempt. The handful of animals that occasionally stand up to men are that much more magnificent. Some day, perhaps, polar bears will race away at the sight of man. But for the glorious present, the polar bear is his equal, unafraid, proud.

When hunting was abolished in Alaska, all research money for polar bears was shut off, and Lentfer was left high and dry. But an exciting change may correct that: Several states now allow a deduction from income taxes for donations to a research fund dedicated solely to nongame species. Colorado in 1977 was the first, followed by Oregon, and next my home state of Minnesota, where it was called the "Chickadee Checkoff." The response was overwhelming, much of it from hunters themselves, who demonstrated that they care about all of nature. Carrol Henderson, supervisor of Minnesota's nongame wildlife, is enthusiastic. "With that fund we now have fifty projects ranging all the way from frogs and toads up to elk," he says. "It's a dramatic change in the course of conservation. No longer is research and habitat improvement dependent on license fees. The public at large can be in on it."

Other states followed quickly: Utah, Kansas, Kentucky, Idaho, New Mexico, Oklahoma, Virginia, West Virginia, South Carolina and New Jersey. Alaska, which has no state income tax, allocated funds from its oil royalties for nongame species.

Another hopeful sign for the future is the sanctuaries being established for bears and other arctic wildlife. Ontario in 1968 set aside a subarctic habitat the size of New Hampshire as a polar bear provincial park, to protect its bears, caribou, foxes, and snow geese. Manitoba is considering a similar park that would include the most important islands and coastal regions from York Factory north.

Russia has set up a refuge on Wrangel Island without major opposition, since the islanders are seal hunters and reindeer farmers who rarely, if ever, hunt bears. Denmark established a national park in east Greenland comprising a quarter of a million square miles where many animals, including polar bears, are completely protected. Such a sanctuary is unique in a country where ten thousand people are almost totally dependent on hunting. A game preserve in northwest Greenland and one in Melville Bay, where denning occurs, are also planned.

Large sanctuaries have also been set aside in Norway's arctic islands, including nearly all known denning areas, which are concentrated on King Karls Land and the north coast of Nordaustlandet, where Kalle once ruled in benign magnificence. Norway reports that from a low in 1970 of around one thousand bears, the population on Svalbard has more than doubled, partly from an increase in cubbing there and partly from immigration from the western Soviet arctic and northeast Greenland.

I would propose a sanctuary that includes magnificent Cape Churchill, with its ancient shorelines and eskers that turn to gold as the sun rises or sets. A few well-placed towers would provide visitors with a vantage point from which to observe the tundra and its bears, its ptarmigans, its snowy owls, and its superb bird of prey, the gyrfalcon.

All nature-loving people should be able to enjoy such a day as I had one October at Cape Churchill. No less than a thousand ptarmigan foraged in half a dozen flocks near the tower, moving like snow flurries as a predator approached. A gyrfalcon sat motionless atop a six-foot willow, eyeing the ptarmigan directly below as they fed on willow buds. One ptarmigan must have forgotten itself and moved from under the safety of the willows, for all of a sudden, the gyrfalcon dived on it. There was a flurry of feathers, but out of them the ptarmigan flew up unsteadily and lit on top of a willow, obviously dazed, I thought, since it chose such an exposed position. But the ptarmigan must have sensed another predator below it, for then there was a flash of red as a fox raced in and leaped all of six feet high, barely missing the ptarmigan as it catapulted straight up. At once the gyrfalcon dived at the fox, and dived again and again as the fox raced across the tundra for cover. Shortly, the gyrfalcon flew to a pile of feathers where in days past it must have made a kill. Now the fox returned and chased it off. The whole performance lasted no more than a single breathless minute.

There have been other memorable moments. On a day in September, a female polar bear and her small cub were crossing the ice of a shallow pond dotted with reeds. The sun was bright, and around each reed the ice had thawed a little, so at each step the mother took, small spurts of water burst from the holes. The little bear stopped, mystified. He took a few steps. The little fountains bubbled. He sat down, obviously puzzled. After a few seconds he rose to his full height of three feet and pounced, slapping the ice with his small paws. All about him, geysers erupted, pure silver in the sun. Again and again he pounced with delight, while his mother waited, looking back over her shoulder from time to time. His enthusiasm for making fountains never diminished—nor did mine—until a soft whoosh from his mother stopped the fun and sent him galloping off to join her.

I would like every lover of nature to know polar bears—not the neurotic creatures penned up in dismally small cages, but bears as the Lord intended them to be, like the cub I watched recently. He was the size of a dog, and he was pushing himself forward on his chin. Then he rolled on his back, kicking his feet in the air. The black pads of his feet were ludicrous, as if he had walked across an inked pad.

So far, much of the arctic is still unspoiled—a land without a beer can. It takes a few days of conditioning until you realize that an object shining in the moss is not a discarded aluminum tab but a flake of mica, a chunk of quartz, or a pool of ice meltwater trapped in the rocks. It takes a while to shake off the debris of civilization, but oh, the rewards! The joy of picking your way across rocks covered with age-old mosses, of walking on a carpet of heather and crowberries and cranberries so beautiful you hardly dare step!

All mankind has a stake in the arctic. For every species of plant or animal we exterminate by accident or design, we diminish the beauty, the excitement, the grandeur of our planet, reduce it to a life of asphalt and golf balls, survival and little else.

How empty the arctic would be without its lordly bears. For me, every encounter with one is brushed with magic; I have the distinct feeling that I have had an audience with royalty. Here is a creature that doesn't shrink from the sight or sound of humans but accepts them as interesting fellow animals.

A big female was buffeting my plastic container of water. I couldn't keep from shouting, "Get away from here." She left it and came up close, fixing her black eyes on mine. "Why?" she seemed to be saying. "What gives you authority over this land?"

Poster from Churchill

POLAR BEARS IN TOWN: WHAT TO DO?

1. Get indoors and stay there.
2. Call the RCMP or Conservation Office.
3. Never harass or antagonize a bear.
4. If no buildings are close by, stay inside your car.
5. Under no circumstances approach a bear on foot.
6. Do not chase or harass bears with your vehicle.
7. If on foot, stay in well-lighted areas.
8. Do not hinder bear-deterrent activities.
9. Children should be driven to and from all locations and never be allowed outdoors at night without supervision. During daytime, children should not play among shoreline rocks.

FOR LEADERS

Always hike in groups.

Carry a noisemaker, such as bells or cans containing stones. Most bears will leave the vicinity if they are aware of your presence. Remember, in dense brush and along rocky shorelines, noisemakers may not be effective.

Leave no food from lunches. Leave nothing but your footprints.

Running is not a good solution. It may invite pursuit.

Bears appear to move slowly, but can make surprising speed over rough terrain.

A bear rearing on its hind legs is not always aggressive. If it moves from side to side it may only be trying to get your scent and focus its eyes.

As a last resort, play dead. Drop to the ground, face down, put your legs up to your chest and clasp your hands over the back of your neck. Bears have been known to inflict only minor injuries under these circumstances. It takes courage to lie still, but resistance would be useless.

Don't take your dog in bear country. Sight and smell of a dog often infuriates a bear and may bring on an attack, and your pet may come running back to you with the bear in pursuit.

Other Bear
Legends

Once a polar bear came roaming inland. It saw an owl sitting on a hummock looking for lemmings. The bear cried out: "Do you sit there, bolt upright, doing nothing?"

The owl answered: "And you tramp about, as usual, with your belly hanging lower than your chest?"

The bear answered: "What do you think you are, you with your round eyes rolling about?"

Just then the owl rose to fly, and as it flew it called: "See if you can catch me."

"Wait for me," said the bear. "Wait for me!"

Once a musk ox lamented to the polar bear. "It is not well to try one's strength against those that live on the surface of the earth, those who have the swift ones to let loose upon us, and have weapons that can spring forth from their hands."

The polar bear said, "Those that live on the surface of the earth are not difficult to strike down with a blow of one's paw, if only one can come at them from behind."

Once an old woman had a bear as a foster child. When it was full grown, people wanted its flesh but the foster mother wanted it to live. When she sent it away, the bear spoke thus to her: "When you suffer want, walk along by the open sea and when you see a bear, call to it." Later, when she began to suffer want, she called to a bear on an ice-floe but it ran away. Every bear did the same until one day a bear rose up on its hind legs, then went to another bear, killed it, and dragged it ashore for her. The people were pleased with her. This is how it was that the one who might have been a provider for the village had to go away because people wanted to kill it.

Once a foolhardy cub decided to hunt the staggerer and bring fame upon himself. When he found a track he lay in wait, but the dogs came upon him and he could not outrun them. Then the staggerer came and thrust a rod into him and he couldn't move. All the while he was skinned and cut up and brought home to be eaten, he was aware of everything. For four days he stayed in the igloo and was given tools, then his spirit could leave and did.

NOTES

Personal

Postscripts

1. We chose to use the term Eskimo, rather than Inuk (pl. Inuit) although in parts of the Canadian arctic Inuk is preferred. Eskimo is a name given by Indians and means "eaters of raw meat" whereas Inuit means "the people."

2. Our apologies to women for using the masculine throughout this book. Except for animals with cubs, identification of sex is uncertain, and "it" seems inappropriate for so massive a creature.

3. It is thought that the bowlegs of many Eskimos come from riding in the packlike *amaut* on their mother's back during the two or three years that they are constantly with her.

4. Nomenclature of brown bears varies. The grizzly is *U. horribilis*. The barren ground grizzly is sometimes *U. richardsoni*; a small, darker kind may be *U. macfarlani*; still others may be *U. andersoni*, *U. inopinatus*, and still more. There is little agreement. Kodiak may be *U. middendorffi*.

5. The first hybrid was born in a small zoo in Stuttgart, West Germany. But at the Washington, D.C. National Zoo in 1936, a male polar bear named Snowy and an Alaska brown, Ramona, produced triplets of exceptional vigor and size: a female, Pokodiak and two males, Taku and Fridgee; three years later, they produced another male, Willie. All were brown with the brown bear's broad head. But in 1959, Willie and Pokodiak produced Elmer, a healthy all-white male, exciting the interest of geneticists. All lived a long time. Willie died in 1972, Pokodiak in 1974 at thirty-eight.

6. Mitchell Taylor, an American biologist, has another theory, that the weights and skull sizes of Alaskan bears are biggest because hunters have gone out by air far beyond the coastal populations that have been heavily hunted. He believes there are bigger differences within populations than between them. Although the biggest male he has tagged was from north of Point Barrow and weighed sixteen hundred pounds, he has tagged several near Radstock Bay that were twelve hundred pounds and some in the Greenland Sea that weighed twelve hundred to fourteen hundred pounds.

7. These icebergs start out life on the northwest coast of Greenland; one glacier—the Humboldt in Kane Bay—stretches for seventy miles along the coast. For a time the icebergs move north, but then turn and start their grand tour south. With so little of their bulk exposed to the wind, they drift slowly.

8. Periodically, newspapers carry accounts of zoo bears with green fur. What happens is that algae take up residence inside the hollow hairs, especially those broad, stiff guard hairs of the flanks, the legs, and the rump, giving the animals patches of green.

9. George Kolenosky, Ontario biologist who has immobilized several hundred black bears in their dens, says that though some are awake, more are groggy and can be drugged without their being aware of what is going on.

10. Grizzlies have comparable reproductive schedules and seem to breed successfully as long as they live. A bottle-reared female on Admiralty Island, Alaska, was still producing cubs at age eighteen.

11. Names of the month are taken from the autobiography *I, Nuligak*. There is little agreement between villages on the names for the months. At Repulse Bay, Octave Sivanertok told me these names: January is *Gangattarsit*, when the sun barely comes up; February is *Ikkarparvik*, when the sun comes up a little higher; March is *Avvunivik*, when seals have young; April is *Tirrigluit*, when seal pups lose their white fur; May is *Nurrait*, when caribou have calves; June is *Munniit*, when birds have eggs; July is *Sugganut*, when caribou lose their fur; August is *Akkuliit*, when caribou fur is half its full length; September is *Ammiraijarvik*, when caribou lose the velvet of their antlers; October is *Ukkiulik*, when caribou fur is full length; November is *Nuliarvik*, mating season for caribou. He could not recall the name for December.

12. It is a marvel that plants and fruit survive in a land where temperatures often plunge below freezing when clouds go across the sun, where precipitation is often less than in many deserts, and where winds may reach a hundred miles an hour and more. The reason they do survive is that they grow close to the ground. Throughout one-twentieth of the earth's surface, no plant grows taller than a few inches. Whether on the mountainous rocks of Baffin Island or the sodden tundra of Alaska and Siberia, the law is this: keep low or perish.

13. Within a month after a caribou is born, short spikes appear, precursors of the antlers that both sexes grow and shed each year. Caribou are curious animals and, like many herd animals, seemingly deficient in brain power. When I got out and stood beside my vehicle in my fur-trimmed parka, they came running over to investigate me, yet later, when Dan tried approaching them for photographs, they took off swiftly. Flies torment them during the warmest part of the day, so they gather on the shore of Arctic Ocean and even on offshore reefs where winds usually blow. At Prudhoe Bay they gather on air strips or empty parking lots and even inside hangars. Numbers of them stand in the shade of the pipeline. Lone animals seem to suffer most from flies, and often you see one race across the tundra as if its life depended on flight, pause for a moment, shudder, shake its head, and go off again. The flies ease off as the sun drops lower.

14. Polar bears thrive in the heat of a Texas summer at the splendid Gladys Porter Zoo in Brownsville, Texas, but on diets that keep down their weight. David P. Thompson, zoologist, says they are among the easiest of animals to keep.

15. The maternity dens of brown bears in Alaska, though similar, are burrows in the earth, sometimes floored with alder and willow branches, and covered with a deep layer of snow. Lentfer in a five-year study of 82 dens on Kodiak Island and the Alaskan Peninsula, found all dens to have a single entry and only one chamber. Most bears seemed to dig a new den each fall, since erosion, seepage and thawing caused the roof to collapse during spring and summer. In one den he found co-occupants, two young bears he assumed to be littermates, denning for the first time without their mother.

16. Cubs in zoos are notoriously hard to keep alive. Perhaps the Nuremberg Zoo has been among the most successful in this respect; between 1945 and 1960, thirty-seven cubs were born, of which nineteen were successfully raised. For a zoo mother to keep her cubs alive requires three essentials: complete isolation in a dark, fairly small area; strict privacy without any human contact, by either sight, sound, or smell; and a period of fasting by the nursing mother comparable to that in the wild.

17. Polar bear cubs are a real zoo attraction. When Marsha of the San Francisco Zoo brought out her cubs for the first time, people jammed the fence rails to see them. When she pushed the cubs into the pool for their first swim, there were tense moments as the tiny bears struggled to keep afloat. Just in time, she dived in and lifted them out, grasping them by the skin of the neck.

18. Unlike polar bears, blacks and grizzlies fight a trap with continuing fury, chewing off trees six inches thick and sometimes digging up piles of rock and dirt. The comparison, however, is probably not fair since foot snares cause little or no discomfort as against the pain of a jawtrap.

19. Accustomed to traveling, polar bears in zoos, especially those confined in small cages, react to enforced idleness no better than a traveling salesman confined to quarters. Some swing their heads from side to side ceaselessly, an action seen only rarely in the wild. Such zoo neurosis is much less common where bears have spacious quarters and a big pool. In fact, zoos find that polar bears are

often top attractions. A big female at the Stockholm Zoo in Sweden liked to drop a bowling ball from a high boulder, then she would dive in and retrieve it, holding it between her nose and one forepaw as she walked out of the water on three legs and climbed to the top of the rock again!

20. Wayne Born is convinced from the stories he heard from his parishioners that polar bears plug up surrounding aglus to increase their chances at the open ones. Stirling cannot believe they do this.

21. Stories have been told of how hunters would wait for a bear to rise to his hind feet, then plant their spears below it so that it impaled itself as it came down, but no Eskimo I talked to ever spoke of a bear rearing up in a charge.

22. Kaludjak had just returned from an eight-day, three-hundred-mile hunt alone by snow machine. A handsome man of about fifty, his curly hair—like that of many others in the Hudson Bay area—suggests ancestry that dates back to the days of whaling ships, many of whose crews were Negro.

23. Rosa's tiny wrists are covered with delicate tattooing from the day when, as a child, she pricked them with a needle and rubbed charcoal into the wounds. The practice was once common. Her teeth are worn to the gums from a lifetime of chewing sealskins to shape them into clothing, but the smile of her warm brown eyes lights up her face as she speaks.

Granny has spent nearly all her life in an igloo during winter and a skin tent in summer. As a child she cared for a polar bear cub so young its eyes were not yet open; she kept it alive until it could run, but then it died. When big bears came near the snowhouse she was terrified and cried aloud, though her mother tried to quiet her, saying she would frighten the bear away.

24. Raw caribou meat, an Eskimo delicacy, is safe and delicious. In most Eskimo homes chunks of it are left in the living room, where family and guests shave off slices with the crescent-shaped *ulu*.

25. Father Mascaret is one of several magnificent priests who have given their lives to the people of the far north, and whose biographies would contribute to the history of heroism and selflessness. As a young man from eastern France, he was dropped off at Repulse Bay. It was four years before anyone returned with mail or other news. He formed an Eskimo cooperative store to which he contributed, among other things, fresh tomatoes, cucumbers, and radishes he had grown under lights. He knew stark poverty. He learned to cut each match in three pieces to make them go further, but never succeeded, as his Eskimo friends did, in cutting them in four. He has shot three polar bears, and from one he had a pair of trousers made, which, he said, were handsome but impossibly hard to walk in. His friends helped him celebrate his first seal, walrus, caribou, and polar bear. He learned to dread the arrival of planes. At Pelly Bay after each plane landed there would be an outbreak of disease. At one time, seventeen Eskimos died of measles.

26. Humans invoke fear in most animals ranging from timidity all the way to terror. It would be hard to say how much—if indeed any—of that fear is innate and how much learned from a parent that has been chased, shot at, snared, trapped, or otherwise mistreated. Behavior of mammals and birds on the Galapagos Islands would suggest that fear of humans and their powerful scent is not instinctive, that animals need to be instructed in the danger. Man, the procreative marvel that he is, has saturated the earth with his species so that few manless spots exist except for barren, distant islands like the Galapagos. Only in the antarctic and perhaps the remotest parts of the arctic have animals lived free of man's intervention long enough to lose any ancestral fear of humans.

27. At Hall Beach, "Ne-ge-lik-ta"; at Holman, "neri lerupta."

28. Stan Price of Admiralty Island, Alaska, knows grizzly behavior as few other people do, and, though he loves them, he considers them brutal with one another. Price has lived for forty years on a houseboat tied up in Pack Creek, where bears come to catch salmon. He and his wife keep two photo albums of Belinda and Susie, whom they bottle-fed twenty years ago. Now the albums are full of photos of the two bears' many descendants. Sometimes as many as forty bears at a time fish in Pack Creek. In his years with them, Price has walked among them with no more than a stick, and has had to use it only twice on strange males that wandered in and did not know him.

Grizzlies fight like cats, with a big swipe of their paws, Price says, and despite all literature to the contrary, they climb trees with ease. A female climbed trees for several days until she finally caught and killed one of his bottle-fed cubs. Females are more ferocious than males. Price is amused at stories of big males chasing men; he believes them to have been females. Shortly before we visited him, two females chewed up a big male. Sometimes females drag a visiting male into the water and try to drown him.

I had no intention of checking out Stan's research, but I suddenly found myself being stalked by one of his females. I had simply (which is the proper word for it!) gone to the far side of the braided creek to watch the salmon struggling upstream in the shallows when I saw a bear and cub that had somehow approached within seventy-five yards—and me without a stick, I thought, my heart suddenly pounding. I walked slowly away from the salmon run. She changed her course to follow me. I knew the grizzly's speed, having just clocked one on the shore of the Arctic Ocean. I knew, too, how retreating figures lure them. So I turned and faced her, motionless. She stopped, sniffed the breeze for five interminable seconds, and then turned back to the stream bank.

29. A barking dog seemed to be what irritated a bear on the north coast of Somerset Island, where a party of geologists was camped. When the bear attacked, one student rushed to a nearby hut for a rifle. The bear seized his companion. The party chief grabbed the rifle but, in his haste, did not slam the bolt far enough forward, and the gun clicked. At once the bear turned to him, knocking him to the ground and trying to bite him on the back of the neck, then dragging him off as a third student carefully aimed, fired, and killed the bear.

30. It is true that the Russians did not hunt polar bears, but they were not above slaughtering their black bears. This story appeared in the *New York Times* under a Paris dateline of 20 February 1965, at a time when Russia was urging a hunting ban on polar bears:

> A dozen Frenchmen, each of them with eight days and $2,500 to spare, have their bags packed for Siberia.
>
> They include some of the expert marksmen of France and they are ready to drop everything and grab the next plane to Moscow just as soon as an Intourist message gives them the signal.
>
> The group is the first to enroll under a Siberian bear-hunting program launched here by Transtours, a travel agency specializing in trips to the Soviet Union and eastern Europe. Transtours is offering bear hunters eight days in the Soviet Union with a guaranteed kill for $1,500.
>
> According to an Intourist spokesman in Paris, the trouble is that Soviet bear production is just not able to keep pace with the demand this year. The hunter who did get out brought back the pelt of a 930-pound Siberian black bear.
>
> Immediately a bear's winter hideaway has been traced by field workers for the Intourist office in Irkutsk, a teleprompter message is sent to Transtours in Paris and the man at the top of the list gets the green light to set out the following day.
>
> A recent exchange between Irkutsk and Paris ran: 'Have animal available, please send hunter soonest.' 'Have you two bears? My hunter has a friend.' 'Regret but recent earth tremors disturbed local bears, only one available at moment.'
>
> Victor Bolchenko, the director general of Intourist, arrived in Paris a few days ago for a brief visit to see how the market in hard-currency bear-hunting was developing.
>
> Russia seemed to have conveniently forgotten that its national symbol is a bear.

31. The term "local people" was settled on because the Alaska Constitution does not recognize ethnic differences—everyone is an Alaskan. Basically, the same applies in Greenland; one is a Greenlander. In practice, most hunting is done by Eskimos and in some places, like Hudson Bay and James Bay, by Indians as well.

32. For his aggressive calls, Wooldridge went to the Olympic Game Farm in the state of Washington and recorded the growls and hisses of two big males that saw each other for the first time. When they fought they mainly shoved with their shoulders. There was no stand-up boxing so common in the play-fighting of polar bears.

33. Wooldridge had hoped to try out the highly publicized "taser," a bullet wired to give a powerful electric shock to anything its strikes, but the device was quickly outlawed after it fell into the hands of criminals.

FURTHER READING

Amedeo, Luigi, of Savoy, Duke of Abruzzi. *On the Polar Star in the Arctic Sea*. Dodd Mead, 1903.

Anderson, William R. *U.S. Polar Expeditions*. "Comments on the Voyage of the U.S.S. *Nautilus*." University of Ohio Press, 1967.

Aristotle. *The Works of Aristotle*. Vol. 4. Oxford, 1910.

Asbjörnsen, P. C., and Moe, Jørgen. *A Time for Trolls*, trans. Joan Roll-Hansen. Dreyer A/S, 1962.

Astrup, Eivind. *With Peary Near the Pole*. Lippincott, 1898.

Azisi, F.; Mannix, J.; Howard; D., and Nelson, R. A. "Effect of Winter Sleep on the Pituitary-Thyroid Axis in the American Black Bear." *American Journal of Physiology* 237 (1979): 227–30.

Barrow, John. *A Chronological History of Voyages into the Arctic Regions*. John Murray, 1818.

"Behavioral Aspects of the Polar Bear." Third International Conference on Bear Research and Management. Bear Biology Association. 1974.

Belikov, S. E. "Data on the Settling Down in Dens of Polar Bear Females on Wrangel Island." Academy of Science, USSR Institute of Evolution, Morphology and Ecology of Animals. 1973.

Brown, R. "Mammals of Greenland." *Proceedings of the Zoological Society*, London 1868.

Bruemmer, Fred. *Encounter with Arctic Animals*. McClelland and Stewart, 1972.

————. *Seasons of the Eskimo*. McClelland and Stewart, 1971.

Congressional Record. *The Polar Bear: Where? How Many?* Proceedings and Debates of the 89th Congress, 1 April 1965.

Cook, H. W.; Lentfer, J.; Pearson, A. M.; and Baker, E. B. "Polar Bear Milk." *Canadian Journal of Zoology* 48 (1970): 217–19.

Cooley, Richard A. "International Scientific Cooperation on the Polar Bear." IUCN Bulletin 2 (7) (1968): 54–56.

Crandall, Lee S. *The Management of Wild Mammals in Captivity*. University of Chicago Press, 1964.

Davis, R. A.; Finley, K. J.; and Richardson, W. J. *The Present Status and Future Management of Arctic Marine Mammals in Canada*. Northwest Territories, Yellowknife, 1980.

DeMaster, D. P., and Stirling, I. "Ursus maritimus" in *Mammalian Species*. American Society of Mammalogists, 1981.

Eertmoed, Elizabeth. "Polar Bears at Brookfield Zoo: A Behavioral Study." Paper prepared for Zoology 356. Chicago State University, 1975.

Erickson, Albert W., and Sommerville, Ronald J. *Annual Project Segment Report*. Alaska Department of Fish and Game. Vol. 5. 1965.

Eskimo Magazine. New Series, no. 1. Spring-Summer, 1971.

Eskimo Stories. National Museum of Canada. Bulletin 235. N.d.

Freeman, Milton M. R. "Polar Bear Predation on Beluga in the Canadian Arctic." *Arctic* 26 (1973): 163–64.

Grojean, R. E.; Sousa, J. A.; and Henry, M. C. "Utilization of Solar Radiation by Polar Animals: An Optical Model for Pelts." *Applied Optics*. Vol. 19 (1980): 338–46.

Hall, Charles F. *Life with the Eskimos*. Harper, 1865.

Harington, C. Richard. "Polar Bears and Their Present Status." *Canadian Audubon* Magazine. January-February, 1964.

———. "Life and Status of the Polar Bear." *Oryx*, Journal of the Fauna Preservation Society. December 1965.

———. "Denning Habits of the Polar Bear." Canadian Wildlife Service Report. Series 5. 1968.

———. "Polar Bear." *Hinterland Who's Who*. Canadian Wildlife Service, 1968.

———. *Proceedings of the Third Working Meeting of Polar Bear Specialists*. IUCN Publications, New Series, supplemental paper 35. 1972.

Jackson, Frederick George. *A Thousand Days in the Arctic*. Harper, 1899.

Jenness, Robert; Erickson, Albert W; and Craighead, John J. "Some Comparative Aspects of Milk from Four Species of Bears." *Journal of Mammalogy*. Vol. 53, no. 1 (1972): 34–37.

Jonkel, C. J. "A Polar Bear and Porcupine Encounter." *Canadian Field Naturalist*. Vol. 82, no. 3. July-September, 1968.

———. "Some Comments on Polar Bear Management." *Biological Conservation*. Vol. 2, no. 2. January 1970: 115–19.

———. *Polar Bear Research in Canada*. Proceedings Conference on Productivity and Conservation in Northern Circumpolar Lands. IUCN Publication. New Series, no. 16 (1970): 15–54.

———. "Of Bears and People." *Western Wildlands*. Winter 1975.

———; Kolenosky, G. B.; Robertson, R. J.; and Russell, R. H. "Further Notes on Polar Bear Denning Habits," in *Bears—Their Biology and Management*. Proceedings Second International Conference on Bear Research and Management. IUCN Publication, New Series, no. 23 (1972): 142–58.

———; Smith, P.; Stirling, I.; and Kolenosky, G. B. "The Present Status of the Polar Bear in the James Bay and Belcher Islands Area." Canadian Wildlife Service Occasional Paper, no. 26. 1976.

Kiliaan, H. P. L. "The Possible Use of Tools by Polar Bears to Obtain Their Food." *Norwegian Polar Yearbook 1872*: 177–78.

Kistchinski, A. A., and Uspenski, S. M. "New Data on the Winter Ecology of the Polar Bear on Wrangel Island." Academy of Science, USSR Institute of Animal Evolution, Morphology and Ecology. 1973.

Knudsen, Brian. "Researching to Protect Our Polar Bears." *Canadian Geographic Journal*. Vol. 90, no. 5. 1975.

———. *Ecology of Polar Bears on North Twin Island*. S. M. thesis. University of Montana, 1973.

Kolenosky, G. B. *Polar Bears in Ontario—Maternity Denning and Cub Production*. Ontario Ministry of Natural Resources, Fish and Wildlife. 1974.

Larsen, T. "The Trapping and Study of Polar Bears." *Polar Record* 13, no. 86 (1967): 589–693.

———. "Capturing, Handling and Marking Polar Bears in Norway." *Journal of Wildlife Management* 35, no. 1 (1971): 27–36.

———. "Polar Bear: Lonely Nomad of the North." *National Geographic*. April 1971.

———. "Air and Ship Census of Polar Bears in Svalbard." *Journal of Wildlife Management* 36, no. 2 (1972): 562–70

———. *The World of the Polar Bear*. Hamlyn, 1978.

Lavigne, D. M., and Øritsland, N. A. "Black Polar Bears." *Nature* 251 (1974): 218–19

Lentfer, Jack W. "A Technique for Immobilizing and Marking Polar Bears." *Journal of Wildlife Management* 32, no. 2 (1968): 317–21.

———. "Polar Bear Tagging in Alaska." *Polar Record* 14, no. 91 (1969): 459–62.

———. "Polar Bear Report." Annual Progress Report. Alaska Department of Fish and Game. Vol. 1. 1970.

———. "Polar Bear—Sea Ice Relationships." Bears—Their Biology and Management. IUCN Publication. New Series, no. 23 (International Conference at Calgary).

———. "Polar Bear Management in Alaska." Third International Conference on Bears—Their Biology and Management. IUCN Publication. 1974.

———. "Agreement on Conservation of Polar Bears." *Polar Record* 17, no. 108 (1974): 327–30.

———. "Discreteness of Alaskan Polar Bear Populations." *Population Ecology of Game Species* (1975): 323–29.

———. "Polar Bear Denning on Drifting Sea Ice. *Journal of Mammalogy* 56 (1975): 716–18.

———. *Environmental Contaminants and Parasites in Polar Bears.* Final Report No. W-17-4 and W-17-5. Alaska Department of Fish and Game, 1976.

———. Statement on Polar Bears with Regard to Marine Mammal Protection Act of 1972. Proceedings of the Seventh Meeting of the Polar Bear Specialist Group. IUCN Publication. 1976.

Lønø, Odd. *Etter Isbjørnen.* Norsk Polarinstitutt, 1954.

———. *The Polar Bear in the Svalbard Area.* Norsk Polarinstitutt, 1970.

Lundberg, D. A.; Nelson, R. A.; Wahner, H. W.; and Jones, J. D. "Protein Metabolism in the Black Bear Before and During Hibernation." *Mayo Clinic Proceedings* 51 (1976): 716–22.

Manning, Thomas H. *Age Determination in the Polar Bear.* National Parks Canadian Wildlife, 1964.

———. "Geographical Variation in the Polar Bear." *Information Canada (Canadian Wildlife Service 13).* 1971.

Metayer, M. *I, Nuligak.* Simon and Schuster, 1966.

Nansen, F. *Farthest North.* Peter Martin Associates, 1897.

Nelson, Edward William. *Natural History of Alaska.* Government Printing Office, 1887.

Nelson, R. A. "Winter Sleep in the Black Bear: A Physiologic and Metabolic Marvel." *Mayo Clinic Proceedings* 48 (1973): 733–37.

———; Wahner, H. W.; Jones; J. D.; Ellefson, R. D.; and Zollman, P. E. "Metabolism of Bears Before, During and After Winter Sleep." *American Journal of Physiology* 224 (1973): 491–96.

———; Jones, J. D.; Wahner, H. W.; McGill, D. B.; and Code, C. F. "Nitrogen Metabolism in Bears: Urea Metabolism in Summer Starvation and in Winter Sleep and Role of Urinary Bladder in Water and Nitrogen Conservation." *Mayo Clinic Proceedings* 50 (1975): 141–46.

———. "Urea Metabolism in the Hibernating Black Bear." *Kidney International* 13, supplement 8 (1978): 171–79.

———. "Protein and Fat Metabolism in Hibernating Bears." *Federation Proceedings* 39 (1980): 12.

Nero, Robert *The Great White Bears.* Winnipeg Department of Mines, Resources and Environmental Management, 1971.

Nordenskiöld, A. E. *The Voyage of the "Vega" Round Asia and Europe.* Macmillan, 1882.

Nunley, Larry. "Successful Rearing of Polar Bears." *International Zoo Yearbook.* Vol. 17. 1977.

Nyholm, Erik S. "On Polar Bear Behaviour in Spitzbergen." *Norwegian Polar Yearbook 1975–76.* 1976.

Oleson, T. J. "Polar Bears in the Middle Ages." *Canadian Historical Review.* March 1950: 47–55.

Øritsland, N. A. "Temperature Regulation of the Polar Bear." *Comparative Biochemistry and Physiology* 37 (1970): 225–33.

———. "A Windchill and Solar Radiation Index for Homeotherms." *Journal of Theoretical Biology* 47, no. 2 (1974): 413–20.

———; Lentfer, J.; and Ronald, K. "Radiative Surface Temperatures of the Polar Bear." *Journal of Mammalogy* 55, no. 2 (1974): 459–61.

———; Ronald, K.; and Jonkel, C. J. "Solar Heating of Mammals: Transmission of Light Through Hairs." 1974.

Peary, Robert E. *The North Pole: Its Discovery in 1909 under the Auspices of the Peary Arctic Club.* Greenwood Press, 1910.

Pedersen, A. *Der Eisbar: Verbreitung und Levensweise.* E. Bruun, 1945.

———. *Polar Animals.* Taplinger, 1966.

Perry, R. *The World of the Polar Bear.* Cassell, 1966.

Rasmussen, Knud. *Across Arctic America.* Greenwood, 1968.

———. *Intellectual Culture of the Iglulik Eskimos.* AMS Press, 1976.

———. *Intellectual Culture of the Caribou Eskimos.* AMS Press, 1976.

————. *Intellectual Culture of the Netsilik Eskimos*. AMS Press, 1976.

Richardson, John. *Natural Sciences in America*. Arno Press, 1974.

Rogers, Lynn. "Shedding of Foot Pads in Black Bears During Denning." *Journal of Mammalogy* 55, no. 3. August 1974: 672–74.

Russell, R. H. "The Food Habits of Polar Bears of James Bay and Southwest Hudson Bay in Summer and Autumn." *Arctic* 28 (1975): 117–29.

Sater, John E. *The Arctic Basin*. Arlington, Va. Arctic Institute of America, 1969.

Scoresby, William Jr. *Arctic Region, with History of Whale-fishery*. 1920.

Seton, Ernest Thompson. *Lives of Game Animals*. Charles T. Branford Co., 1909.

Shereshevski, E. I., and Petriaev, P. A. *The Polar Bear Manual of the Arctic Hunter*. Moscow, 1949.

Sivak, J. G. and Piggins, D. J. "Refractive State of the Eye of the Polar Bear."

Smith, Pauline; Stirling, I; Jonkel, C.; and Juniper, I. "Notes on the Present Status of the Polar Bear in Ungava Bay and Northern Labrador." *Canadian Wildlife Service Progress Notes* 53 (1975).

————, and Stirling, I. "Résumé of the Trade in Polar Bear Hides in Canada." *Canadian Wildlife Service Progress Notes* 66. August 1976.

Smith, T. G. and Stirling, I. "The Breeding Habitat of the Ringed Seal (*Phoca hispida*): The Birth Lair and Associated Structures." *Canadian Journal of Zoology* 53 (1975): 1297–305.

Stefansson, V. *Hunters of the Great North*. Harcourt Brace, 1922.

————. *My Life with the Eskimo*. Macmillan, 1913.

————. *The Friendly Arctic*. Greenwood, 1943.

Stirling, I. "Vocalization in the Ringed Seal (*Phoca hispida*). *Journal of Fisheries Resource Board* (Canada) 30 (1973): 1592–94.

————. "Midsummer Observations on the Behaviour of Wild Polar Bears." *Canadian Journal of Zoology* 52 (1974): 1191–98.

————. "Polar Bear Research in the Beaufort Sea." *The Coast and Shelf of the Beaufort Sea*, edited by J. C. Reed and J. E. Sater. Arctic Institute of America, Arlington, Virginia. 1974.

————. "Polar Bear Conservation in Canada." *Canada's Threatened Species and Habitats*. Canadian Nature Federation. 1977.

————. "Biological Importance of Polynyas in the Canadian Arctic." *Arctic* 33 (1980): 303–15.

————, and Jonkel, C. "The Great White Bears." *Nature Canada*. Vol. 1, no. 3. 1972.

————; Andriashek, D.; Latour, P.; and Calvert, Wendy. *The Distribution and Abundance of Polar Bears in the Eastern Beaufort Sea: A Final Report to the Beaufort Sea Project*. Fisheries and Marine Service, Department of the Environment. Victoria, B.C. 1975.

————; Archibald, R.; and DeMaster, D. "The Distribution and Abundance of Seals in the Eastern Beaufort Sea." Journal of Fisheries Research Board of Canada. 1975.

————, and McEwan, E. H. "The Caloric Value of Whole Ringed Seals in Relation to Polar Bear Ecology and Hunting Behaviour." *Canadian Journal of Zoology* 53 (1975): 1021–27.

————; Pearson, A. M.; and Bunnell, F. L. "Population Ecology Studies of Polar and Grizzly Bears in Northern Canada." *North American Wildlife Conference* 41 (1976): 421–30.

————; Schweinsburg, R. E.; and Kiliaan, H. P. L. *Polar Bear Research Along the Proposed Arctic Islands Gas Pipeline Route*. Progress Report to the Environmental Management Service, Department of the Environment, Edmonton, Alberta. 1976.

————, and Archibald, W. R. "Aspects of Predation of Seals by Polar Bears." *Journal of the Fisheries Research Board of Canada*. Vol. 34, no. 8. 1977: 1126–29.

————. Jonkel, C.; Robertson, R.; Cross, D.; and Smith, P. "The Ecology of the Polar Bear along the Western Coast of Hudson Bay." *Canadian Wildlife Service Occasional Paper 33*. 1977.

————, and Latour, P. B. "Comparative Hunting Abilities of Polar Bear Cubs of Different Sizes." *Canadian Journal of Zoology* 56 (1978): 1768–72.

————; Schweinsburg, R. E.; Calvert, W.; and Kiliaan, H. P. L. "Population Ecology of the Polar Bear Along the Proposed Arctic Islands Pipeline Route: Final Report to the Environmental Management Service." Department of the Environment, Edmonton, Alberta. 1980

134   *Further Reading*

————, and Kiliaan, H. P. L. "Population Ecology Studies of the Polar Bear in Northern Labrador." *Canadian Wildlife Service Occasional Paper 42.* 1980.

————; Calvert, Wendy; and Andriashek, D. "Population Ecology Studies of the Polar Bear in the Area of the Southeastern Baffin Island." *Canadian Wildlife Service Occasional Paper 44.* 1980.

————, and Cleator, Holly, eds. "Polynyas in the Canadian Arctic." *Canadian Wildlife Service Occasional Paper 45.* 1981.

Thoren, Ragner. *Picture Atlas of the Arctic.* Amsterdam, 1969.

Tovey, P. E. and Scott, Robert F. "A Preliminary Report on the Status of the Polar Bear in Alaska." Presented at the Eighth Alaska Science Conference. 1957.

U.S. Department of the Interior and University of Alaska. *Proceedings of the First International Meeting on the Polar Bear.* 1966.

————. *Administration and Status Report of the Marine Mammal Protection Act of 1972.* 1976.

Uspenski, S. M., and Chernyavski, F. B. "Maternity Home of Polar Bears." *Prioroda* 4 (1965): 81–86.

————, and Kistchinski, A. A. "New Data on the Winter Ecology of the Polar Bear on Wrangel Island." IUCN Publication. New Series, no. 23 (1972): 181–97.

————; Belikov, S. E.; and Kupriyanov, A. G. "Polar Bear Research and Conservation in the USSR: 1975–76." *Proceedings of the Sixth Polar Bear Specialist Group.* IUCN Publication, 1977.

Van de Velde, F. "Nanuk, King of the Arctic Beasts." *Eskimo* 45 (1957): 4–15.

————. "Bear Stories." *Eskimo.* New Series, no. 1 (1971): 7–11.

————. *Eskimo's Mensen Zondertijd.* Van Holkema & Warendorf, 1981.

Vibe, C. "Arctic Animals in Relation to Climatic Fluctuations." *Meddelelser om Grønland* 170, no. 5 (1967).

We Don't Live in Snow Houses Now. Canadian Arctic Producers Limited, 1976.

Wemmer, C. "Design for Polar Bear Maternity Dens." *International Zoo Yearbook 1974.*

————; Von Ebers, M.; and Scow, K. "Social Behavior of Captive Polar Bears with an Emphasis on Mother-Young Interaction." Unpublished paper.

————. "An Analysis of the Chuffing Vocalization of the Polar Bear." *Journal of Zoology* 180. London, 1976: 425–39.

Wenzel, G. "Inuit and Polar Bears: Cultural Observations from a Hunt near Resolute Bay, N. W. T." McGill University. Unpublished paper.

Wilson, D. E. "Cranial Variation in Polar Bears." IUCN Publication. New Series, no. 40 (1976): 447–53.

Wooldridge, D. R. "Chemical Aversion Conditioning of Polar and Black Bears." *Proceedings of the International Conference on Bear Research and Management.* 1977.

————, and Belton, P. "Natural and Synthesized Aggressive Sounds as Polar Bear Repellents." *Proceedings of the International Conference on Bear Research and Management.* 1977.

NOTE: Manitoba Department of Renewable Resources has several publications on the arctic, including *Taiga, Tundra and Tidal.* N.d.

Also, Parks Canada, Ottawa, has a series of brochures on Banks Island, Ellesmere and Axel Heiberg islands, the Pingos of Tuktoyaktuk, Northern Yukon, Wager Bay, and Bathurst Inlet. 1978.

INDEX

135